SELLING
USABILITY
USER EXPERIENCE
INFILTRATION TACTICS

John S. Rhodes

SELLING
USABILITY
USER EXPERIENCE
INFILTRATION TACTICS

Rhodes Media
2009

Selling Usability:
User Experience Infiltration Tactics

By John S. Rhodes
Copyright © 2009 Rhodes Media

This book was printed in the US

Cover and interior design by:
Danil Mullagaliev
danil.kazan@gmail.com

1st Printing March 2009

To the greatest man that I'll ever know, my father. He put criminals in jail but they would thank him for his courtesy. He'd give these men some dignity during their dark and difficult times. They would shake his hand out of pure respect. And, get a load of this: Just remove the gun and badge and you're left with gentle and caring grandfather. Seriously, what more could a son ask?

Contents

THE BASICS

PEOPLE

THE INFILTRATION TACTICS EXPLAINED

CLOSURE

INDEX

1

Who, Why, Wha?

Read, every day, something no one else is reading.
Think, every day, something no one else is thinking.
Do, every day, something no one else would be silly enough to do.
It is bad for the mind to be always part of unanimity.
~ Christopher Morley

I always read the last page of a book first so that if I die before I
finish I'll know how it turned out.
~ Nora Ephron

End Here

Let's start with a definition. User experience (UX) is the overall experience and satisfaction a person has when using something. The product, service or system in question should allow the person to meet their goals while satisfying business and functional requirements. Good UX is a good thing, bad UX is a bad thing.

This book will tell you exactly how to get UX into an organization. I wouldn't be writing this book if it were easy to get this done. It's a difficult, uphill battle.

User experience professionals face three challenges:

- 99% of the people in an organization are not thinking about UX and the other 1% are thinking about women, fire and dangerous things.

- Most managers understand UX about as well as they understand the average airspeed velocity of an unladen swallow.

- Being involved in UX is an open invitation to getting beaten about the head and neck by grandmothers, hamsters, celery, and co-workers.

If you are a user experience professional the problem isn't that you lack skills, rather it is that you can't get others to understand the value of what you do. I'm not going to help you sell UX and I'm not going to help you justify it to others. Instead, I'm going to help you sneak it into an organization. We're going to be working on the sly.

You're a smart puppy but you probably don't have a portfolio of methods to slip UX into a company. This book is full of stealth. We've got guerilla attacks, end runs, and cloaking devices. These tactics are not conventional.

I'm asking you to reject the frontal assault. We'll be successful under the radar. By the way, I'm not suggesting anything unethical or devious. We'll be a bit Machiavellian but we won't do anything that will make you feel greasy and queasy. We're looking for victory behind the scenes, not the dead weight of guilt.

To sum it up, we're going to focus on what the business cares about: business. This is the UX MBA. Rather than focusing on UX, which you already know, I'm going to drag you into the business world. I'll help you understand "their" language and "their" rules. I'll help you focus on business and profits first, then UX. Everyone is going to benefit.

Why Are You Reading This?

I'm assuming that you truly enjoy UX. You believe user experience design is the right way to get things done. You can easily talk about usability, information architecture, human computer interaction, human factors, interaction design, ergonomics, and user centered design. You know that these things have roots in psychology, philosophy, anthropology, and sociology. Focus on people first, right?

It is possible you are just starting your career in UX. It is also possible that you are a UX veteran or a manager of UX professionals. Perhaps you are a consultant looking for ways to improve your business. No matter your role in the UX world, you are going to better understand the relationship of user experience to business and vice versa.

I do think that the world has changed for the better regarding UX. There are many strong organizations and groups ready to support you (e.g., HFES, CHI-Web, SIGIA-L, AIGA, UPA). There are many more jobs in UX now. I see "usability" in job postings, advertisements, and product descriptions. UX has also made a splash in a few large companies such as Microsoft and IBM.

Despite these gains, UX is still hardly known or understood by most people. It is under funded. It is improperly labeled as quality control, design, and marketing research. How many times have you heard that a usability test is really just a marketing test? The horror never ends. That's why you're reading this book.

I'm going to make your life easier. You'll be able to better position UX in your organization and increase your job security. I'm going to make you feel more comfortable with business topics. We'll integrate UX with profits but most folks won't even know it. You'll benefit from this. You'll be recognized, just as you deserve. Of course, everyone is going to benefit because we know that UX is good stuff. It is hardly a punishment or problem for organizations.

Why Do I Think I've Got the Answers?

I'll start by saying that I'm the guy behind WebWord.com, which is one of the oldest blogs on usability and user experience. I've been feeding people with UX information for over 10 years.

I've also done UX with, and for, several organizations including IBM, Women.com, Cabelas, US WEST, Binghamton University, Universal Instruments and Lockheed Martin. If it matters to you, I also have a B.S. in Management Science, an M.A. in Philosophy, and an M.A. in Experimental and Cognitive Psychology.

The summary is that I've been around UX for a while. I've been reading and writing about it for longer than most folks. I've written hundreds of articles and I've conducted many interviews with UX experts.

On the flip side of the UX story, I also understand business and technology. For example, I've been a business analyst and webmaster. I supported sales, service and marketing organizations for years and years. I've been a software engineering manager in charge of nearly 20 direct reports and multi-million dollar budgets.

The short story is that I suffer from the Better World Syndrome. That is, I want to make the world a better place. UX can make the world a better place. To me, usability is not a joke. It can save lives, ease pain, enable the disabled, and more. I believe in it. So, by helping you I am helping the UX cause. This stuff matters to me.

How Does the Book Play Out?

It is pretty straightforward, really. I believe in short, easy to read chapters. I'll give you a summary of the chapter and then supporting material. Each chapter will have examples or little cases studies. Despite the fact that I'm going to give you tons of help and advice, you should be able to read this book in just a few hours. You can chow it down on a plane ride from New York City to Los Angeles.

I'll end this introduction by saying that I'm really excited about this material. I drink the user experience Kool Aid and I love it. You can rest assured that I will help you as much as I possibly can through this book. If you've been beaten down, don't worry. We're going to make some magic happen.

2

The First Business of Business is Business

Business exists to supply goods and services to customers,
rather than to supply jobs to workers and managers, or
even dividends to stockholders.
~ Peter Drucker

It's not personal, Sonny. It's strictly business.
~ The Godfather

Summary

Businesses care about the bottom line. The focus is on customers and profits. You need to realize that businesses generally operate without any consideration of UX. At a minimum, it is certainly not the center of the universe. Money is magic whereas UX is merely one tiny, little piece of the picture. All of these things mean that you cannot force your ideas on businesses. It is hard to win a frontal assault. To get UX into a company you need to operate in stealth mode.

Splish Splash

Brace yourself. I am throwing a colossal wave of cold water on the UX torch that you carry around. This might hurt a little.

If you are like me, you really care about user experience. You care about human factors, ergonomics, usability, user-centered design, information architecture, and all that other great stuff. You have a deep, sincere empathy for users. If you are like me, you truly enjoy UX and everything it stands for. You care about users, you like research, and you like to help other people. You're hip on UX. Maybe you're in love with UX.

Unfortunately, most folks in business don't think like this. The bad ones merely think about themselves and maybe profits. The good ones usually care about customers and profits. Not UX.

Stop Drinking the User Experience Kool Aid

UX is a lifestyle. I wear it on my sleeve. You might be this serious too. However, this is dangerous for us. It makes us targets. Thinking of UX first and business second will get you crushed. Nearly everyone else working with you is certainly not thinking of UX. So reverse your thinking. In terms of the appropriate business perspective, profits come first and UX comes second.

This doesn't mean that you should give up on UX. I'm not suggesting that any more than I'm suggesting you give up food, air and sex. No, instead I'm suggesting that your role in the business is to focus on how to help the business through UX. It is a tool. It is a means to an end. The bottom line is the bottom line.

You should not try to sell UX any more than you should try to sell mathematics or critical thinking. It is a way of getting things done. Your job from this point forward is to understand how businesses can benefit from UX. Understand how it is mechanism to drive profits and help customers at the same time.

How Do You Talk About UX?

The advice I am going to give you next is worth the price of the book: Do not talk about user experience for at least a month. Instead, before you say or do anything regarding UX, think about what it means to the bottom line. Modify your language to be more in line with the true intentions of the business. Below are two examples.

Example One

> What you want to say: "We need to better group and categorize the content on the top of the second order page to allow for more whitespace. That should improve readability which we know users have complained about due to our latest help desk feedback."

What you should say: "Customers are having issues that decrease sales by 38%. We can fix this with a couple of changes that will take about four weeks to complete. The breakeven on this effort is less than four months."

Why better? First, I've used the word customer instead of users. Business folks understand exactly what a customer is. Second, I've made a direct connection to business issues and benefits. Third, I've made very concrete, measurable claims.

Example Two

What you want to say: "A recent usability test indicated that 17% of users do not understand how to enter the discount code. Furthermore, they indicated that the entry field is too short and should be larger. We are confident that the results are statistically significant given the sample size and experimental design."

What you should say: "We know that customers can't figure out how to enter discount codes on our web site. I reviewed this with our sales team; we're losing about $24k per month. They also indicated that we're at risk of losing 10% of our customers permanently. I spoke with the design team and we can fix this problem for $80k."

Why better? Once again, I've used the word customer instead of users. I've made this point twice now because it is so important. Second, I barely talked about the problem. Instead, I talked about the impact of the problem on the business. Third, I avoided jargon where possible. Most folks don't care about statistical significance. Finally, I deliberately put this problem in the context of the sales team. What they say, do and think is extremely important to the rest of the business.

Summary of infiltration tips

- Understand that UX is not the center of the universe.
- Don't try to sell UX, instead focus on the benefits of UX.
- Work with sales and marketing to understand how UX fits.

3

User Experience is an Ugly Baby

In the modern world of business, it is useless to be a creative original thinker unless you can also sell what you create. Management cannot be expected to recognize a good idea unless it is presented to them by a good salesman.
~ David M. Ogilvy

Babies are always more trouble than you thought and more wonderful.
~ Charles Osgood

The Birth of UX

User experience was just born in the last couple of decades. Donald Norman used the term "user experience" in User Centered Systems Design (1986) and then again in What You See, Some of What's in the Future, And How We Go About Doing It (1995). From there, it gained some traction. It really started to take off in the late 90's. Although somewhat useless in meaning, I did a search for "user experience" on Google: 44 million results. Not too shabby.

Before declaring success, and despite my definition earlier in the book, I need to tell you that user experience isn't exactly the most effective term in the world. There is an insane focus on users. Are they people? Are they customers? Are they participants in a research study? Similarly, what kind of experience should we expect from user experience? What is the goal or the drive of that experience? When you combine these two words into one concept – user experience – we're in for serious trouble. I'll sum it up for you in one word: confusion.

So, UX is a relatively new concept and it is also somewhat confusing and vague. That's a recipe for disaster in the business world. If we can't define the damn thing how can we even think about selling it? How can we expect managers and co-workers to accept it? This is exactly why a frontal assault simply will not work. Getting UX into an organization through direct approaches is doomed.

Put yourself in the shoes of a manager. If you have $50,000 to spend on improving a product in the marketplace, are you going to spend it on this mysterious "user experience" or instead on quality, advertising, or engineering?

The Story Gets Worse before it Gets Better

Most folks involved in UX do not have business or management experience. This means that few people can bridge the gap between the two worlds. There isn't a common language available. This leaves UX at a disadvantage.

Another thing that I've noticed is that UX professionals tend to be business passive. That is, they don't tend to focus on business or profits as an objective. In the UX world, there seems to be a focus on theory, purity and research. There is a focus on practical results too, but that focus is in a bubble which isn't tied to profits.

How to Substitute and Reinforce

You are in a tough spot. It is rare that managers and executives "get" UX, which makes life a serious challenge. Unless these folks understand and embrace UX, money and security will not follow. Without money and security, you will never be in a good position in your organization. Budgets will always be tight. Your job will always be on the line.

You might think that I am using scare tactics. You might be right. But, I've worked with enough organizations to know that UX is tough to sell. The best way to get it into an organization is to fly it in under the radar. That's why you're reading this book.

Summary of the chapter.

- UX has only been around for 25 years; it isn't ingrained yet.
- UX isn't well defined, so business folks can't stand behind it.
- Most UX professionals are not aggressive about business.

4

Understanding Your Role in the (Dis)Organization

Freedom is just chaos, with better lighting.
~ Alan Dean Foster

*What is necessary to change a person is to change his
awareness of himself.*
~ Abraham H. Maslow

Business Isn't Clean, Neat or Simple

There's a common belief that companies are neatly organized and structured. In a big company, you have a good idea about who sits where and who does what. You know your boss and your boss's boss. The hierarchy is usually pretty obvious. You also know when the paychecks are cut, how to make travel plans, and how to file your TPS reports. The bigger the company the more you'll see the pyramid and the ladder to the top.

All of these things make you feel warm and comfortable. Like you, I've felt the embrace of the Corporate Mother. But we shouldn't be fooled. Just because we see and feel structure, we can't assume that everything is perfectly planned or well built.

Business is a messy affair. Deals are constantly being brokered. Workers ("resources") are constantly shifted from one project to the next. Managers are constantly searching for ways to increase productivity. Add this up and you'll realize that there is a lot of flexibility.

Sure, there is structure, but there is also a lot of wiggle room. Business is dirty and with UX you can clean up. You can increase the structure and order. The better you can define and structure work, the better off you'll be because with clarity you reduce risk. Managers hate risk; they love people who can reduce it. In business, there's nothing so valuable as a sure thing. Put that idea in your pocket and never let it go.

Know Yourself, Know Your Skills

Before you play the trumpet of risk reduction, you have to understand how you fit. You have to assess your skills, particularly you UX skills, and know what you can do for an organization. Remember, your value isn't simply what you can do in terms of a card sorting session or heuristic review. Instead, the literal outcome of your UX work is the value you add. And, one step beyond that, when you have answers, you can sell risk reduction.

Let's walk through that again. First, you have to think about the UX tools you have at your disposal. Second, after cataloging these tools, think about how they benefit the company and the customer. Finally, instead of telling your manager about the tools or outcomes, you instead talk about risk reduction, increased productivity or customer satisfaction.

The key in this stream of activity is to first understand what you really offer the organization. List out every single UX tool that you have at your disposal. Make sure you really know what you can get done. Then, take the time to list out all of the true outcomes of that work. Why is that usability test useful? What does it offer your company, your manager, or your customers?

Know the benefits of the work you do. You simply have to know yourself and your skills. If you don't, you can never sell yourself or your skills. Many chapters in this book depend on you taking the time to catalogue and understand why you really get that paycheck as a UX professional. It is far less obvious than you might realize so burn some cycles on figuring it out.

Embrace Change, Movement, Gaps and Problems

Business is messy and cluttered and landmines are everywhere. But, that is actually good news for you. Consider for a moment that you cannot ever have an impact if nothing is changing. Change is your friend.

Here's an analogy. If a stock stagnates, you can't make money. If the price goes up or if the price goes down, you can profit. You can buy and hold, you can speculate, you can sell short, and much more, and still profit handsomely. But, if the stock never moves it is really tough to make money unless it is throwing off serious dividends. In the same way, if projects stand still you cannot have an impact. However, if the project is on the rise, you can increase the chances of success. If it is falling, you can save the day. In sum, change is good. This is true with stocks and this is true with UX.

The key to success is to recognize the changes in your projects and organization. Then, with your UX toolbox in hand, you can swoop in with answers to the tough problems. You can increase product quality, decrease project risk, and reduce support costs.

You need to start getting in tune with the ebb and flow of projects. You need to talk to people about the star projects and the lame dogs. Again, look for change. Look for those nasty problems and gaps. You'll find that many projects can be improved by getting an injection of UX. Match the benefits of various UX methods to the business problems that organizations face.

Force of One

I usually work alone. If you're like me this means that most of your time is spent heads down. In turn, you're probably not focused on business events in the organization. This has been the case when I've done consulting and when I've worked inside large organizations. At the same time, I find that I need to communicate with the business folks on the UX activities going on. They want updates.

This reporting feels like a hassle. "It's just paperwork." Most of this activity probably is a waste, but it is your chance to get face time with key decision makers.

In terms of UX infiltration, consider yourself a conduit between managers and the other UX professionals in your organization. If you are literally working as the sole UX force in your company, then start thinking about how you can help the business. Take the business perspective. Feed their minds with UX at every opportunity. The more you are on your own, the more this matters. Extra support is crucial.

Here's a useful exercise. If you needed to justify your job to your company, what would you say and what would you do? Would you talk about tools and methods or would you talk about the value you add to the company? What value do you really add?

Taking this one step further, I suggest that you take your salary and multiply it by five or, even better, ten times. That is the amount of money you need to save or generate for your company. After overhead, taxes, depreciation, attrition, training, and so on, that isn't unreasonable. You're employed by an organization to make money or help others make money. It takes a lot of time and money to make money.

My final advice is to think of yourself as being in business for yourself. If you are a consultant, that's like falling off a log. But, if you are a UX worker bee, start thinking like a consultant and you'll be 184 steps of every other UX professional out there.

If you're still thirsty for more, don't fret. I'm dedicating an entire chapter later in the book to the consulting mindset. Rock on!

Summary of infiltration tips

- Business is messy but UX outcomes provide clarity if sold right.
- You have to take time to understand the business value of your UX skills if you expect others to buy what you're selling.
- Change is good and gaps are opportunities; stagnation is bad.
- Always consider that your job is on the line; you should always think of yourself as a consultant.

5

Users: They Don't Really Count (gasp!)

User is a term used for only two groups of people in the world:
computer operators and drug addicts.
~ Michael Martine

Banana banana banana terracotta banana terracotta
terracotta pie
~ System of a Down (Vicinity of Obscenity)

Summary

While users are critically important in the world of UX, it is in your best interest to avoid using the term user around others. Most folks in your organization won't grasp the true meaning. Put yourself in their shoes to understand the possible confusion. Focus instead on using business friendly substitutions for user, such as customer. There are plenty of places to hunt in your organization to get further inspiration. If you insist on sticking with user you need to slowly inject it into the culture until it is accepted.

Why Users Don't Matter

Obviously users matter. To you, that is. If you care about user experience you obviously care about users. That's the idea, right? Users come first.

Unfortunately, the idea of users is foreign to most business folks. Take their perspective for a moment. We extract data from users. We don't train them. We don't help them. They don't buy anything from the company. Why should they matter?

Please realize that I'm talking about the term user versus the role of a user in research. Obviously we have users and we love them very much. But, how we convey our interaction with users to managers is dearly important to slipping UX into organizations.

Language Matters in Business

So, try not to use the term users if you can help it. At the same time, I do encourage you to talk about customers and others that interact with your organization. There is nothing wrong with explaining how people outside the company drive the success and profitability inside the company. You can certainly slip in comments about how you are working with these folks to improve your products and services. Maybe even discuss research and testing, but just don't take it too far or you'll be wandering too far into the UX world for their comfort.

If you do talk about users please talk about them in terms of business results you are generating. It is better to talk about customers and markets, of course. Just keep in mind that your reference to users is analogous to a finance manager talking to you about convertible subordinated debentures. Not good.

If you don't agree with my specific advice, I understand. At least understand that you need to take it slow and deliberate. They key is baby steps. If you go hog wild throwing around the term users you are attempting a frontal assault. You might not get the mileage you desire.

The Ways Out

As previously mentioned, it isn't terrible to mention users or participants when talking about literal research. Being practical, those conversations typically make folks outside UX glaze over already. Managers and co-workers expect you to use jargon. Unfortunately, this won't exactly help you sneak UX into your organization.

I like talking about customers instead of users. It seems to work better than just about anything else. I also like talking about potential customers and future customers. That is very effective with management, but also sales and marketing.

One of the best ways to figure out the right language for users is to talk to folks around your organization. Find out how they refer to people outside your organization. Start to sniff around the marketing and sales departments, as well as engineering and product development teams. It is possible there is a term that everyone uses that makes sense when you talk about UX topics.

I've also found that there are some folks that are really curious about UX. There is no good way to know when lightning will strike. When you do get traction take advantage of it. Be a little more aggressive about using the term user as well as other UX terms.

Summary of infiltration tips

- Users are wonderful, but don't use the term user.
- Using the term customer or future customer works better.
- Focus on the benefits of working with customers.
- If you find folks that are interested in UX then talking about users is relatively safe; consider injecting other UX terms into these conversations but take it slow.
- To find other ways to talk about users, talk to sales, marketing, engineering and the product teams.

6

Managers: Keeping Track of Bean$, Frank$ and Bill$

What do you need from me in order to kick ass on this project?
~ Scott Berkun

Then you find your servant is your master...
~ The Police (Wrapped Around Your Finger)

Summary

Most managers are tasked with keeping track of budgets. They work on many things and with many people. The focus is on money; they count the beans. Managers are also tasked with managing human resources. The point is that they are not thinking about users and user experience. They don't understand users and UX but they can make or break you.

Managers Are People Too

Most managers do not dream about user experience. It's not on their minds. Ever. This isn't anything against UX; it is just human nature. They're thinking about their families, their bills, and everything else.

Managers are not all the same. Don't fool yourself. They have their own interesting backgrounds and hidden biases. Joe's boss is different than Sally's boss. Consider yourself lucky if they even know a drip about UX.

I've worked for mangers with deep financial knowledge, others with serious technical firepower, and still others that were project management wizards. One of my managers liked to ride snowmobiles and another liked to gamble. People are people.

Take the time you need to get to know your manager. What makes her tick? What makes him happy? What language does she use? How does he think about your projects? Get these answers. Learn what you can about your manager so that you can better align UX with their point of view, language, and personal zeitgeist.

Improve Your Manager's Life

All managers that I know are under constant stress. The Dilbert version of the world, while often quite funny, doesn't match up with what I've seen. Perhaps I've just worked with and for some really great people.

The reality is that most managers are under time pressure. Budgets are usually tight. Managers also have to deal with a lot of risk.

Fortunately, you can provide your manager with help. If you know anything about UX then you know that you have the ability to increase the likelihood of project success. Tons of research indicates that UX decreases costs, decreases risk, decreases cycle time, and improves quality. Simply find the right place to ply your wares.

What I'm getting at is pretty simple. Consider how UX is good for your manager versus you or your customers. UX can sponge up buckets of stress and risk. Use it to help managers improve their game.

Leverage What You Know

Many people forget that managers have managers. They have their own bosses and their own obligations.

If you think of your manager as your internal customer then the directors and vice presidents are definitely some of your targets too.

That is to say, you need to figure out what your management chain wants and needs.

Find ways to help your manager succeed in the eyes of others in the organization via UX. Provide your manager with tools, tips and techniques that demonstrate risk reduction and improved quality. Be sure your materials can be easily passed along to others, especially those people up the food chain in your organization. If your stuff is good you never know where it might go.

Money and Budgets

Nearly all managers care about budgets. Money is on your manager's mind. It has to be because if it isn't they will fail.

You can take advantage of this focus by demonstrating how UX can drive down costs. For example, I've done usability tests for exactly zero dollars. I've designed simple tests and completed some pretty useful usability work on no budget. There is always time involved but otherwise you can't beat the cost if you do it right.

If you save the company money and you produce results, be sure that management finds out about it. This is just the kind of thing that your manager needs to understand. This is how UX will make its way into your organization. Results matter.

A final bit of advice about working with your manager is to learn more about budgets, finance and accounting. Spend some extra time learning the language of business, especially around the topic of profits and the bottom line. This will help you better position UX on your projects and with your manager.

Quick Advice for Managers

If you are a team leader or manager, you have a lot more leverage than average employees. If you are interested in UX, nearly all of the advice in this book will help you.

You can hire UX thinking employees. You can send your team to get usability and information architecture training. You can buy books on user centered design and interaction design, then pass them out. There's a lot you can do. I'm sure you're seeing that.

Summary of infiltration tips

- Find out what managers think about so you can relate it to UX.
- You can decrease a manager's personal stress through UX.
- Demonstrate how UX decreases project risk and lowers cost.
- Learn the language of business: money.

7

Customers: The Most Powerful User Experience Friends

If you work just for money, you'll never make it,
but if you love what you're doing and you always
put the customer first, success will be yours.
~ Ray Kroc

Okyakusama wa kamisama desu
~ Haruo Minami

Summary

Businesses need customers but customers don't need your business. There are always alternatives and options. Once you understand that all business depends on customers, you understand why customers are more important than management and your co-workers. If you win customers over using UX, perhaps by removing some pain they feel, you will keep them happy and your organization will thrive. But, if you extend your reach and get them throwing UX back at your company, you achieve a much more glorious victory. Help them speak for you; they are thermonuclear powerful. It is absolutely true that this is the ultimate way to get UX into your organization. Win the customer and you win the game.

Customers First

Without customers the business world stops. You need customers to buy stuff from your company. You need them to buy stuff so that your company can make a profit and provide you with a job along the way. To be even blunter, without customers your life stops. They indirectly feed you, provide you with clothing, put the roof over your home. Customers allow you to fill up your iPod with music and they make it possible for you to purchase that caramel swirl cappuccino with whipped cream and cinnamon dust.

Most people working for The Man don't really think of things this way. However, the folks making the most money understand this very well. Sales, marketing and management all understand that customers make the business world spin. Also, they will listen to customers before they listen to you. Anything stated by a customer is about 44,278 times more important than what you say.

This stuff is crucial to understand because it indicates exactly where and how to spend your time. Rather than trying to make you point again and again and again to your management or your peers, you can spend your time working with customers. Not only will you better understand what they want and need, but you'll establish a rapport with them. This will allow you to get them talking about UX. If this happens, then inevitability they will start expecting UX from your organization and it'll have to react. This will be good for everyone.

It is important to state again that customers are not equivalent to users. A customer buys stuff from your company whereas users are the folks in your interviews, cognitive walkthroughs, and card sorting tasks. Customers pay for stuff produced by your company whereas you give users money for data. Customers can be users, but only when you are doing research. Keep this distinction clear in your mind, but more importantly in your language.

User Experience is Pain Medication for Hurting Customers

Many customers suffer. They simply cannot get what they want when they want it. They don't feel sexy. They don't feel satisfied. They don't feel powerful. They don't feel happy.

Nearly all purchasing is based on emotion. Your job is to figure out what drives that emotion. This doesn't mean you're looking to be manipulative. Instead, you want to be looking for ways to help the customer be emotionally satisfied. Help deliver a quality product with solid usability, but figure out the emotion behind the purchase.

To find the pain points, seek the places that customers quit, drop, skip, or stop. Find this in the marketplace, in your company, or directly from the customer. Don't feel bad about using anyone's data. Engineering, marketing, quality control, sales, and customer service will all provide inspiration and guidance if you just ask.

Don't be afraid to take a road trip to a sales office or a customer site. Sit in the customer service center for a day. Just remember, your worst customers can be your greatest source of data. Keep digging and find the right customers and the right pain points.

There is a good reason to think and act this way. Each customer is a person. Think about establishing a rapport and get to know every customer possible. If you do your job well, you'll get unsolicited testimonials. The key message here is that testimonials about UX from a customer are insanely powerful. With little encouragement or perhaps with an open request, a customer will offer up a quote about UX that will rock your world. Each quote you get is a crowbar that can easily pry doors open. You can move mountains with the right words from the right customer.

On one of my large government projects, I was able to figure out why my primary customer contact was looking for a major victory. It was because he was trying to secure a promotion! The success of the project was tightly coupled to his personal achievement which is not uncommon.

As the project played out, I made it blatantly clear that the little victories we experienced along the way were directly tied to our usability testing, one-on-one interviews, and Help Desk ticket analysis. I made certain that "user experience" came up several times per week; appropriate yet subtle. After a few weeks, the customer used the term with his superiors, my peers, my management team, and everyone else. When the project came to fruition, the main success driver was easily identified by the customer: UX. In turn, this drove many other UX initiatives in the organization.

Passionate Involvement

The advice above might sound a bit more reactive than it really is. You don't have to wait to make the magic happen with customers. Every time you interface with a customer you have an opportunity to discuss or demonstrate UX. Your web site and your help desk are two good examples of this. Also, remember that your products and services demonstrate your organization's commitment to user experience.

If you can engage with your customers, you have the opportunity to establish the rapport we discussed previously. In turn, you can position yourself between the customer and company. This allows you to feed the customer UX stories and it allows you to present the customer's perspective of UX back to the company. In effect, you can tell the UX stories that your customer is telling. This is especially effective if customers are literally talking about the benefits of interaction design, ergonomics, human factors, or ethnographic research. However, it is still best when the customer is speaking the words.

I have found several great ways to interact with customers and in turn, get them talking about UX. My favorite tactic is to co-author articles with them. It's infectious. They can write a little or a lot. They can provide the examples and they can provide the case studies. Along similar lines, I know that some UX consultants have worked with their customers to create in-house seminars. All in all, this type of customer interaction is exactly the way to drive UX into the organization.

The last thing I'll say is that your customers sometimes have customers. If this is true for you, the tactics above are especially important. You can work with your customer's customer which allows you to push and pull UX from more angles. If that end customer is talking about UX, your direct customer will naturally talk about UX to your company. It's completely natural. It's also an extremely effective way to get your company to focus on UX.

Summary of infiltration tips

- What a customer says is more important than what you say, so help them talk about UX when they talk to your company.
- Get customer testimonials relating to UX which you can share with the people in your company.
- Remove pain and help each customer personally succeed via UX; they'll remember you for it and they'll talk to others about it.
- Co-author an article with a customer to get them more involved in UX activities, which in turn you can share with others.

8

Consultants: Wisdom from a Briefcase

I'm more convinced now than ever before that insiders are not the best people to explain a product or service that they've created. They're not the best people to write about it; they're not the best people to market it.
~ John Koetsier

A man with a briefcase can steal millions more than any man with a gun.
~ Don Henley

Summary

Consultants have power, influence and access. That's serious leverage. You can work with them to get UX into your organization. Sincerely try to help them and they will help you without asking. Spend time with consultants when they arrive and also as they work their magic. You might have the opportunity to reach just the right people in your organization in return. Finally, try to stay on top of what is going on in the consulting world. The right consultants will have a keen awareness of UX issues. If you have any part in the decision making process, you can bring in a consultant that exactly fits your needs and the needs of your organization.

What is the Nature of a Consultant?

A consultant is nothing more than an expert who applies special skills, or can provide advice on a particular topic. They offer an organization their talent in return for cash. Nearly all consultants are paid for their brainpower either directly or indirectly.

Consultants are in an interesting position in relation to you and the rest of the employees of your organization. They are highly paid, they are outsiders, they are known to have mad skillz, and they don't stay around too long. They also have a special status, particularly among those in management. There is a perception that consultants have truly special powers and they can make or break a project, so many people pay very close attention to their words and deeds.

This is where UX enters the picture. Your mission is to work closely with the consultant to determine how UX intersects with their work. When the consultant speaks you would like nothing more than for the phrase "user experience" to blow into the ears of management and your peers.

This isn't as difficult as it seems because many consultants play a trick on organizations. What they do is come to an organization, listen to what everyone says, and then say the same stuff back to the organization. This isn't evil. Consultants don't literally mimic others and few of them are puppets. But, very often the same ideas flowing out of the organization simply flow back in through the consultant. There is a tacit agreement among all parties that this is the way to get the job done.

If you're in the mix early while the consultant is still surveying the corporate landscape, you can push your UX agenda in just the right ways. You'll get a lot of mileage out of friendly conversations, documented case studies, and hands on walkthroughs. Don't try to be manipulative. Just try to get a good amount of face time upfront and inject UX as you go.

Feed your thoughts and suggestions on UX topics as the consultant is cooking along making the magic happen. In the case of coding, designing, and development, this works especially well particularly if the consultant isn't too savvy about UX. The key is to help the consultant succeed by using UX methods and tools. Then, if all goes well, the consultant will point out the UX special sauce to your peers and management team. Maybe you'll get some mojo for your efforts.

On one of my major projects about two years ago I was working with an insanely smart, hardcore developer. He happened to be on a long term contract with us as a consultant. He was able to code just about anything. It was impressive to watch him and it was a pleasure working with him. We constantly talked about UX, which just happened to be one of his weaker points. On a regular basis I passed along advice and research reports. There was virtually no UX budget, so I did a ton of coffee cup and hallway usability testing for him. It was a smashing arrangement and eventually, because of our efforts, we did get a reasonable budget to do some usability testing. He was instrumental in making this happen because management saw his outputs. He made it clear that UX made the diamonds sparkle.

The Echo Chamber

A consultant has power nearly equal that of a customer. There isn't quite as much juice flowing, but it can be pretty damn close, especially since your organization is probably paying this person hefty sums of cabbage. At the same time the influence of the consultant doesn't last too long. They don't stick around so their power fades into the background. Nevertheless, when you've got them around and they can talk about UX, get them on your side. Remember: temporary but powerful.

Consultants usually have direct links to management, senior leaders, and key engineers. They have pipelines to top talent and they work with the key influencers in your organization. Indeed, many consultants are brought in explicitly to bend the ears of these people. When you combine the access with the power consultants have, there is serious leverage. My message to you is to ride their coattails.

So, there are actually two messages here. First, get in good with consultants and try to inject UX into their language. Get them thinking about UX so they talk about it with your leaders. Second, if you can't directly influence a consultant, at least recognize that they have open access to leaders and you can likewise gain access by working in their shadows. This obviously gives you the opportunity to throw user experience into the mix of the conversations. Ultimately, this is about leverage. Consultants have power and access.

Lurking in the shadows of a consultant can really pay off. Several years ago I was working with a guy who was an executive trainer. For what it's worth, many consultants are labeled as coaches and facilitators. Don't overlook them. In any event, we hit it off and we ended up eating lunch with each other for about 3 weeks straight. On one of those days we talked in great depth about personas. As we left the lunch area he invited on the fly to be a "guest speaker" on the topic. This put me in front of the entire senior management team for more than 20 minutes where I had the chance to talk about the appropriate use of personas, case studies, and ethnographic research. It was a beautiful thing.

Selecting of the Wizards

You don't go to Amazon.com to pick up a consultant. You're not going to find one at the corner drug store either. Because consulting is usually expensive and topic specific, there is usually a selection committee or at least a selection process. Many times the hands on employees are invited to provide some level of input. Use this as an opportunity to bring in a consultant with a UX orientation.

To do this effectively, you need to maintain your own list of consultants. Stay in touch with these hired guns for your sake and theirs. It'll keep you fresh in many ways. Also, watch their web sites and read their books. The overall message is to network with people that you would like to have inside your organization. You never know when you might have the chance to bring UX into the organization through a consultant. Follow the Boy Scout motto: Be Prepared.

Summary of infiltration tips

- Work through consultants to inject UX into your organization.
- Talk early and often about UX when consultants are ramping up.
- Network with consultants; know which ones understand UX.
- Be prepared to help your organization select the right consultant.

9

Designers & Developers: These Bees Give You Honey

The top 5% of programmers probably write 99% of the good software.
~ Paul Graham

Programming today is a race between software engineers striving to build bigger and better idiot-proof programs, and the universe trying to build bigger and better idiots. So far, the universe is winning.
~ Rick Cook

Summary

Designers and developers get work done. They have direct, tangible impact on the UX of a product through their deeds. This is especially true if they are involved with the user interface in some way. Help them by driving a good set of requirements so they can concentrate on putting together sweet designs. Promote their work while also taking heat when issues arise. Also, keep a wide view of design and development, and take a long-term perspective on your interactions with these miracle workers. Finally, find ways to help people through documentation and the use of patterns.

Heads Down, Hands On

I like almost all designers and developers. The reason is pretty simple. Unlike so many workers, these men and women get real work done. No amount of planning and thinking will make code appear in a library or coax a wireframe to manifest itself on the screen. Designers and developers pound keys and push pixels; they make the rubber meet the road. I thank them from the bottom of my heart.

I know that other people get work done, but when it comes to creation, you just can't beat a designer or developer. I often lump engineers in this group too, and sometimes I'll throw in savvy technical managers, but that is rare.

In a world so full of consumers, designers and developers are wonderful producers. This is critical because UX simply cannot happen until users actually have something to experience, unless they suffer from delusions.

I'll make my point another way. Designers, developers and engineers are translators. That is, they translate requirements into real stuff, which you and I can touch and feel and experience. Their understanding of the world becomes our understanding of the world, no matter what the specification dictates. These fine people are modern day craftsmen, shaping and bending reality.

It is the translation that they do that is so important to our UX activities. If you can help designers and developers understand requirements from the customer's point of view, you can help them create a product that customers will enjoy. Done right, their translation will be more in line with your vision of a great UX. This is an infiltration tactic that has deep, serious and lasting value.

Taking Bullets

In my experience, and based on a quick informal survey, designers and developers don't seem to enjoy interacting with customers and managers. In contrast, most UX practitioners are quite the opposite. They enjoy interacting with people, particularly customers and end users. The obvious way to help designers and developers is to act as buffer. Designers and developers are yin whereas UX practitioners are yang. Understand this dynamic and play it right so that everyone wins.

The second way to take bullets for designers and developers is to do grunt work. Although I don't exactly enjoy paperwork, I see it as an opportunity to inject UX ideas all over the place. By writing reports, writing memos, taking meeting minutes, and so forth,

I can shape things to include UX. We'll cover some of this later but the point is that you need to find ways to help designers and developers because it helps you. It also naturally builds goodwill.

Take Long Term View

Most of the programmers I know don't quickly warm up to other people. They tend to be serious, quiet, logical, introverted, and thorough. This is a bit of a generalization but I think it is mostly true. Indeed, all programmers I know have a least one or two of these personality characteristics. Ultimately this means that you should take your time getting to know these key players. Aim for small, repeated victories. Consider the bigger picture and the long haul.

I've been more successful winning over one developer at a time versus whole development teams. I usually seek out the strongest developers first and then help them as much as I can. The top dogs are always looking for ways to improve their game and UX can be their special edge. In turn, these folks will drip feed their knowledge to junior developers, including the UX tricks they've learned. From a practical standpoint, the best developers are naturally the most successful so it is smart to be aligned with them.

Keep in mind that programmers and engineers are highly motivated by intellectual challenges. That is, they like to master their domains, attack the hardest problems, and break though tough barriers. Design and development is extremely creative despite the common view to the contrary. In light of this, you can position UX as a secret weapon since most developers and engineers don't know much about it.

Clearly demonstrate how UX can help save time and energy, which ultimately prevents burnout. According to various reports, around 50% of development time is spent correcting defects and bugs. What I have done a few times is clearly demonstrate how UX can decrease bugs, which translates to more free time.

How to Keep UX on Their Brains

Designers and developers are intensely focused so it can take some work on your part to break through. Stick with it. Continuously provide UX tips, tricks and research. I've found great success in passing along articles written by developers on topics like usability and focusing on customers. Articles written by respected peers are extremely valuable and they come along a few times per year. They're very much like UX testimonials. I maintain a little library of them which I pass along when the opportunity is right.

It is also a good idea to work with the development team to create a development library, which of course will include several books and articles on the topic of user experience. There are plenty of good books by Nielsen, Krug, Cooper, and others to pass along to developers.

You might also consider setting up an exclusive blog or a wiki for the development team. The intent is to get the troops to rally behind certain ideas, including usability, information architecture, user centered design, human computer interaction, and so forth.

Designers, developers and engineers love patterns and reuse. They really don't like to reinvent the wheel. So, while building your library and setting up your online collaboration spaces, be sure to inject UX patterns. This includes easy-to-use testing methods, simple interview tools, interface design best practices, and pointers to UX sites such as the HCI Bibliography, SIGIA-L mailing list, Boxes and Arrows, and so forth. I'm sure you can think of plenty of others.

I'm working on a project right now where we are taking this action. Interestingly, the programming team has asked me to take a leadership role in this activity since I've been able to demonstrate the value of UX on a couple of large and successful projects. For what it is worth, we do intend to keep this pretty exclusive by keeping out managers, which drives up the perceived value. The developers and engineers involved feel like they're setting up a club. That's pretty interesting but not too surprising. Different teams drive different outcomes. Talk to your programmers and engineers. Dig a little to figure out what will work best in your situation.

Summary of infiltration tips

- From a UX perspective, find ways to help designers and developers translate requirements.
- Protect and insulate programmers and engineers to win their trust while simultaneously showing them the value of UX.
- Do dirty grunt work for developers, such as documentation, to help them but also so you can add UX spice to the artifacts.
- Help the development team build a library, and consider setting up online collaborative environments, all of which will include several UX goodies.

10

Sales:
The Force!

*To get rich you need to get yourself in a situation with two
things, measurement and leverage. You need to be in a position
where your performance can be measured, or there is no way to
get paid more by doing more. And you have to have leverage, in
the sense that the decisions you make have a big effect.*
~ Paul Graham

Life itself is a matter of salesmanship.
~ Thomas J. Watson

Summary

Salesmen are rockets. They are full of energy. Unfortunately, most
of them don't know much about UX so they can't be evangelists. To
sell it they need to know about it, but they need to know how it will
help them make more money. Your trick is to get to know the key
members of your sales team. Try to go on sales calls with them when
possible so you can learn more about your customers, and learn how
the sales take place for your organization. You can help them and
they can help you. Together with your sales team, and with UX as a
pillar of strength, you can help your customers succeed.

They Need to Know About It Before They Can Talk About It

Sales people talk. They talk to a lot of people and they talk all the time,
mostly to product managers, marketing, and of course customers.
Although unusually biased, these workers have an exceptional grasp
of what your company has to offer and what your customers want
and need.

It is really important that you get to know a least a few sales people. It is best to get face time when they are also interacting with customers, either in person or on the phone. This can be quite a trick but the payback is huge.

You can get invited to go along on a sales call if you are privy to unique knowledge or if you have special skills that are valuable on a sales call. Find ways to add value to the sales cycle. And, find ways to help the sales person get even more face time with customers. It is hard to have too much face time in the world of sales.

Here's an example. I was on a team focused on redesigning an external web site a few years ago. In an effort to get some much needed data, I arranged several site visits through a local sales engineer. I explained how the team would utilize the pluralistic walk though method. I made him very comfortable with the approach and I also showed him our testing materials to make him clearly understand our intentions. More importantly, I provided the salesman with an opportunity to make a very friendly sales call with no strings attached. He was able to very clearly explain to the customer that the team was gathering data to make the company web site more customer friendly, which made the company look good. It really put him in a good light; he was able to do some suave marketing. That's the name of the game.

By the way, this activity also provided me with another wonderful opportunity. I was able to schmooze with one of the top sales people in the organization. In turn, and without asking, he told many other people about our UX work. The word spread.

It is 1,000 times more powerful to have a respected sales person spread the word about UX than it is for you to do it. It is also more in line with the general philosophy outlined in this book: keep it simple and keep it under the radar. Others will do work for you without asking when they see the value.

By the way, the data we gathered from the exercise above was fabulous. Yowza! Better still, I was able to inject UX into the company through another person. This guy was a powerful information sneezer with clout and respect. This activity paid dividends for a couple of years straight. Give it a try.

Cult of Personality

As I indicated above, sales people are chatty and outgoing. They're also charismatic, or at least energetic. This means it can be challenging getting their attention so that you can talk about user experience. Then again, the best sales folks are great listeners.

So that's the story. You have to know the people you're dealing with, and how they operate. Get a feel for their communication styles and their way of business and you'll be golden. If you're into UX then you already have a streak of empathy. Apply it and reap the rewards. If you're curious about applying your skills in unique ways, don't worry. We'll talk more about it later in the book.

Big Dogs

Based on what I have seen and what I've read in many sales books, just a few salesmen drive the major portion of sales. Make no mistake: A small set of superstars is radically better than the majority.

If possible, align yourself with these rock stars. There are two good reasons for this. First, these folks have something special. Maybe you can learn some of their tricks. It is possible to find new ways to interact with users and customers. Second, the top sales people are recognized as such. Management listens. If you can get them talking about UX you'll have far more leverage with executives than you'll get with the salesmen at the bottom of the totem pole.

By the way, it is crucial to remember that the sales team is highly motivated by sales. They are motivated by money. The best salesmen are extremely focused on revenue and profits and commissions, but almost always in respect to delivering value to customers. At the same time, this focus has less to do with greed than it does with winning a game. It is the thrill of the kill that drives these folks. Money is how they keep score!

So, when you're talking with these star destroyers, be sure to talk about end user value particularly as it relates to sales. Come back, again and again, to the things that make life better for customers. Demonstrate how UX translates to bottom line value. To this point, you'll never have a better audience to explain how a usability test can constrain total cost of ownership. These guys are tuned into this stuff. Take advantage of it when you have the face time.

One step away from customer

The next best thing to talking to a customer is talking to a salesman. He is just one call away from the people that ultimately make your life possible. You owe your job to your customers but also the sales force. I realized this several years ago and it really opened my eyes up. It also greatly increased my respect and gratitude for the folks on the front line. I saw that my life was possible because of their great work.

If feasible, spend enough time with the sales team so that some osmosis takes place. That is, you can learn a lot about UX from the sales force just by spending time with them even if you aren't peppering them with questions. It probably won't be refined or clean knowledge, but it will be raw and it will be real.

By the way, this knowledge will help shape your own UX activities, including the development of personas and usability testing scenarios, for example. Similarly, you can really learn a lot about market trends. This a fabulous way to get a big picture view of your company and your customers.

You can also get insight on things that would otherwise be hidden from you. I remember being on one sales call where the salesman told me that the clean and smooth look of the product was a key driver of success. I didn't understand this until I asked some pointed questions. I found out that a super clean, super efficient look was highly valuable to some customers because they constantly had streams of people walking through their manufacturing plants. The look of the machines actually mattered more than the output in several instances. Go figure, right? I would have never known this without spending time with the sales team.

Summary of infiltration tips

- Get to know some salesmen, particularly the best ones, so that they learn about UX and start talking about it.
- Go on sales calls to learn more about your customers and to learn new ways to interact with customers; get customers talking about UX if possible, with the permission of sales.
- The language of sales is money; feel free talk about UX in terms of money with the sales team when it makes sense, e.g., reducing total costs or increasing sales conversion rates.

11

Steamrollers: CEOs and Executives

An executive is a person who always decides; sometimes he decides correctly, but he always decides.
~ John H. Patterson

The most dangerous strategy is to jump a chasm in two leaps.
~ Benjamin Disraeli

Summary

It is no surprise that you can achieve great influence in your company if you can get the support of the chief executive officer (CEO) or vice presidents of your organization. They wield insane power. But unfortunately for UX professionals, opportunities for communication with senior leaders are limited. Furthermore, CEOs are hardly thinking about UX and their priorities are skewed away from UX practitioners. To gain traction, it is usually necessary to have others deliver the message to CEOs. There is a need to enlist the help of the sales force, product teams, and middle management. In addition, customer quotes are useful, along with the delivery of targeted UX metrics.

Influence and Decision Making

Nearly all employees in an organization are in the business of persuasion. Middle managers are particular slaves to negotiation because they have enough resources to get some work done but not enough to get it all done. The worker bees are generally busy pounding keys, taking calls, and getting work done, but they also care about influence and persuasion.

On the other hand, CEOs don't worry too much about persuading others inside their organizations. They are in charge, calling the shots. They are consumers of persuasion, but also facts, reports, numbers, and feedback. They listen to customers, the sales force, product teams, and a handful of other senior leaders. Taken as a whole, CEOs and senior vice presidents are busy thinking about strategy, making decisions, and getting the job done from a pretty high level.

There's a very important point in all of this, namely that user experience (UX) information that starts moving toward a CEO needs to be clear and extremely valuable. You want to deliver something that people can easily pass up and along to other people. After all, this information needs to withstand several layers of critical review from lower level managers, through senior leaders. Facts and details are wonderful, but you have to deliver a persuasive UX message. You have to find ways to hit the gut of the CEO. You have to stir emotion.

In all of this, it is likely you'll have to set your ego aside. If you seek personal glory as your UX message moves closer to the CEO, you might be in for a rude surprise. As people become exposed to your high quality information, they'll make it their own, either on purpose or accidentally. If your goal is to obtain personal credit, this could be a bitter pill. Instead, if you stick to the goal of getting UX into your company irrespective of the path, this could be a beautiful victory.

The Q3 Presentation, Debt, and Ball Bearings

CEOs live in a different place than most people. Consider that they have to tolerate hundreds if not thousands of little voices inside and outside the company. They have customer issues to resolve and they have interviews lined up with Wall Street analysts. They have issues you haven't considered and you probably never will.

For example, imagine that from 9:17AM to 10:40AM, the CEO and three senior product managers need to handle a serious quality problem with titanium ball bearings made by a new Chinese supplier. The issue is causing output to drop by 14% on a key product line, which in turn is a million dollar per week headache. What does this have to do with UX? Nothing, and that's the point.

There are some lessons in that last paragraph. First, consider that your slice of the pie is pretty small. No matter how big UX is to you, it simply cannot be everything to a CEO. It cannot be everything to a company. UX is very important but it isn't the center of the universe, especially for senior leaders in an organization. Second, CEOs tend to focus on customer issues. They care about numbers and the big picture. They generally do not have time to dig into details so your summarizations become their details, which is why ROI arguments regarding UX can be so powerful. Third, CEOs are decision makers and problem solvers. They hardly relax. If UX can offer relief, find a way to help. The challenge is moving the answers from your brain to theirs.

The Host and the Parasite

The best way for a flea to get into a home is on the back of a dog. The pooch is a welcome family friend. He goes outside, hangs out, goes about his business, catches a flea or two, and the heads back inside.

The analogy is that CEOs work closely with customers, product teams, senior leaders, and the sales force. If you can piggyback your UX message on the backs of these players, your "flea" will make it into the house of the CEO. Remember, the senior leaders spend a lot of time with these leaders. If done right, the UX message becomes a beneficial parasite, adding value.

What Would You Say?

It is difficult and rare for a UX practitioner to get face time with a CEO or senior executive. So when it happens, it has to be good. Their focus and attention span is limited. Therefore, the language you use, including your sales pitch, must include certain trigger words and business language that reflects their wants and needs. Brevity is critical.

Daniel Szuc of Apogee Usability Asia recently explained to me how the time with a CEO might break down based on his own experience. About 25% of the time is spent gaining confidence, 25% more of the time is spent getting legitimate focus, and the final 50%

on the UX content itself. This pretty much matches up with my own experience with company executives. That is, 50% or less of your time will be spent on the actual UX content. The rest of the time you're establishing a rapport.

What does this mean in the real world? If you only had two minutes of time, you've got about 30 seconds to make a great first impression. You've got another 30 seconds to focus the CEO or executive on the presentation at that moment, and about 1 minute to deliver the core UX message. Again, you need to focus on the UX value proposition but you also need to appeal to the emotions of the CEO. Remember, you're making a sales pitch.

If you are lucky, and you've done a solid job in the first couple of minutes, you'll be able to jabber on for a bit longer. You might be able to make a bigger impact but don't count on it. Overall, the central advice when working with the CEO the first time is to make a good personal impression and provide a high impact overview of the UX work at hand. The bottom line is that if you can't make an impact in a short amount of time, it is unlikely that you'll make an impact at all. Practice your elevator speech.

The first meeting should be the platform for future meetings. All future meetings should be treated as seriously as the first. CEOs and executives are always busy. Always.

How to Make the Most of Your Time and Their Time

Many years ago when I had my first chance to talk with a company president about UX, I was very lucky. After doing a pile of great research our team had ascertained several key insights. However, instead of completely focusing on that data, I decided the president would want to hear what his customers were saying about the company web site, which was the topic at hand.

"Our customers said WHAT!?"

Empirical data is wonderful but customer feedback, particularly testimonials and user quotes, is the way to get immediate focus. CEOs want to understand customers. If you can help them in this way, they don't care if you're a UX practitioner or a dolphin trainer. They care about the results that you deliver. Data is great and I recommend fully leveraging it, but also go for the gut using what you know.

Mind Reading

Executives require rapid solutions to highly diverse and challenging business problems. Your job is to find ways to adapt UX to the needs of your organization in this respect. The senior management team is looking for tools to make financial decisions, determine marketing approaches, develop new products and services, create strategic plans, and make all around good organizational decisions.

UX can mitigate risk, reduce legal liability, and provide CEOs with the warning signals they care about. UX methods can also be used to determine customer loyalty, market position, and product innovation.

In effect, you can help CEOs and executives read the minds of customers and users. In turn, you can solve many of the business problems your leaders care about.

In several other chapters of the book, we'll investigate these things. For now, just recognize that what you know about user experience has high business value. Prepare now for your interactions with senior leaders so that you can strike when the opportunities manifest.

Summary of infiltration tips

- Don't mess around; provide CEOs with key UX information in a clear and effective manner so they can make the right decisions.
- UX is not the center of the universe to CEOs and executives.
- Senior leaders never have enough time, so plan accordingly.
- Customer quotes are worth their weight in gold to CEOs.
- UX has true business value that senior leaders will recognize.

12

Teams: What Mamma Didn't Tell You

Among the IT professionals on today's more innovative development teams are people you wouldn't normally expect to find: psychologists, social scientists and, of all things, users.
~ Miryam Williamson

A creative man is motivated by the desire to achieve, not by the desire to beat others.
~ Ayn Rand

Summary

If you have the time and energy, take a leadership position on your teams. This provides you with access and control. You can divert resources, if only time, to UX efforts. You can educate the team on the value of UX along the way. Most teams are vague blobs of activity. Your peers are starving for organization and structure. Step up to the plate. Show that you have moxie. Demonstrate the obvious value of UX; illustrate the value of user feedback, reduced training costs, high impact documentation, and so forth. Translate the value of UX into terms a diverse team will understand. Also, if you really cannot get financial support to do testing, enlist the help of the team. Innovate with the help of the crew at your disposal.

Great Teams, Great People

There are many types of teams. For example, there are organizational teams, project teams, ad hoc teams and product teams. There are also friendships and relationships that functionally translate into teams. In every case, teams are social constructs, which means that they are based on human relationships.

All great relationships are based on trust. You can build trust by being truthful, and by treating others with fairness and respect. Honesty and patience will take you a million miles when dealing with your peers. You can also build trust by helping others, which is relatively easy to do if you can pass along good UX information.

It almost goes without saying that great teams are made from great people. It is very difficult to achieve victory without smart, creative, enthusiastic people. Fortunately, you can help other people by helping them understand customers.

Helping the Team Satisfy Customers and Users

Teams solve problems and overcome challenges. There's a unified sense of purpose. One weakness of teams is that they are only as smart as the information they are processing. However, if you provide them with key data, they'll be more likely to understand what they are trying to achieve. When the problem space is clearer, the solution is clearer.

Teams often lack key information about customers and ultimate end users. There tends to be a lot of focus on products and services versus the people making purchases and using the goods. That's where you come in. Your skills and your knowledge can help crystallize the team. You can help them rally around a common goal: great user experience.

How to Persuade the Team

It is important to remember that humans make snap judgments but they also have evolving relationships and shifting feelings. For some team members it can be tough to really, deeply understand the value of UX. I've seen this many times with developers "in the weeds" as well as senior managers. Don't expect instant results. Instead, treat every interaction as an investment in the team.

In my experience, the best way to help your team understand the value of UX is to show them a portfolio of tools and data. That is, demonstrate various UX tools and methods, then show them the data, then show them the final outcomes. This really amounts to showing them how the research is performed and the final products. Customer quotes are useful for this as well as before and after demonstrations. The same tactics used by late night infomercials are surprisingly effective when trying to influence how others view UX.

In the past, I've also influenced my coworkers by incorporating usability goals right into the core of the projects. There are two ways to do this. First, you can help others think about the requirements from an outsider's perspective. You can define the problem space or the end user goals in light of the project goals in such a way as to guarantee the use of UX methods to achieve success. Second, you can help define the metrics used to define success. By wording things in the right way, the team suddenly has to rally around certain metrics that drive UX into the project. For example, you might require 90% or higher user success on a several key functions on your new product.

Focus on People but Also the Situation

Groups should be considered in context. Specifically, there is a tendency to think of groups as collections of people. Yet, humans behave in certain ways in light of other people as well as the environment. Group performance happens in light of the structure and context within which groups operate.

This is important because it implies that you can greatly influence groups in light of your own actions and reactions, but also by developing a great environment for UX activities. It means you can set up situations which positively reinforce the use of usability data, iterative tests, ethnographic research, card sorting, and so on. You can make your cubicle or office a haven for people looking for answers to really hard questions. We all know that UX can be used to pry loose the golden answers from the project ore.

As a specific example, I've often used a simple tactic: send team members useful articles that relate to UX. I keep my ears open for problems that are related to users and customer experience, and then I send along research reports, articles, and books to solve those problems. Naturally, this provides me with an opportunity to inject UX into my projects with minimal effort. I can create the right context for UX conversations or I can wait for the situations to present themselves to me. Either way, the context drives the injection of UX in my team. This is less of a frontal attack than trying to win over teammates through direct, out-of-context conversations.

Another simple and obvious tactic is to offer to do "free" usability tests. The idea is to do some level of simple UX research for the folks in your group. Give them help through the research and the data. This is a solid plan as long as you don't come off as offering to critique the work. To get UX into your organization, it is better to show others how the process works and how it benefits the team than it is to be known as a guru. If you fall into that trap, you're only providing fish, and you're not teaching others why it works and how to do it.

Most Leaders Are Not Managers

The people with the greatest influence, power, and intelligence are often far away from management. Likewise, many leaders are regular workers with some special edge. Some leaders are only leaders for short bursts of time, perhaps regarding some topic or some project, or even just a single conversation.

This is potentially quite profound if you realize that as a UX professional, you might have the opportunity to alter the thinking of your team or the direction of the project. Leadership situations are all around, grab them when the advantage is apparent and you can inject UX as it makes sense. The trick is to watch for openings and jump in with both feet. Be prepared with the UX magic dust.

As a leader you can influence an entire group or just one person. Context matters of course. Again, don't bother with abrupt actions unless it really makes sense. Instead, aim for culture change. Invest the time and energy to lead the team to the right place. Ensure that your team is being productive and effective, and then help the team take advantage of situations that are favorable to UX. Take care of the basics first, then inject UX unless of course UX is the answer.

Summary of infiltration tips

- Find ways to gain trust through UX research, data, and solutions.
- Encourage the team to rally behind UX as a common goal.
- Incorporate UX into requirements and metrics; guide the focus.
- Create a positive environment for UX to be discovered, dispersed and discussed by the entire team; create the context for UX.
- At some point in time, you'll be a leader so use the opportunity to wedge UX into the right spaces.

13

Stakeholders: Delivering Money and Power

You can get everything in life you want if you will just help
enough other people get what they want.
~ Zig Ziglar

Learn to help people with more than just their jobs: help
them with their lives.
~ Jim Rohn

Summary

A stakeholder is any person with a stake in the success or failure of a project. Very often stakeholders control the money flowing into a project. They can be champions or detractors. They are catalysts, driving a project to new heights or slamming it into the ground.

Success for Others is Success for You

We've discussed many types of people and how they matter in the quest to get UX into your organization, including groups and teams. However, there is still a list of people that we haven't discussed. Rather than trying to dig into every nook and cranny, I'm going to generalize a bit in this chapter.

Ultimately your success depends on other people. The success of other people will drive your success, often in ways that you can't foresee. Likewise, your customers, peers, and managers are your support network. You cannot easily succeed in a vacuum, especially in a large organization.

I cannot stress enough that all success is personal. Therefore always frame the success of your project in terms of success for those people around you. Success for stakeholders is not a lofty concept. It is about everything from putting food on the table to feeling like a rock star. It is very real, very human.

Two Types of Stakeholders

Stakeholders can be put into one of two buckets. On the one hand, a stakeholder can affect the outcome of a project. On the other hand, a stakeholder is a person affected by the project. A stakeholder has influence or they are influenced.

It is important to know if the person you're working with cares more about creation or consumption. This will help you see the project through their eyes. It will help you understand their assumptions and their goals. It will give you the empathy you need to tailor your UX work to their needs and to their success in the project.

This is more important than it might seem at first glance. If the stakeholder is a creator then UX methods matter very much. On the other hand, if the stakeholder is a consumer then UX attributes matter more. To be blatantly clear, a UX method would be something like a remote usability test, pluralistic walk through, or card sorting task whereas a UX attribute would translate to an easy to use product, higher quality widget, or easier to sell service.

Your peers will tend to care more about UX methods while managers and customers will care about UX attributes. The simple reason is that UX methods help your peers get their jobs done. That translates to their success through a job well done. On the other hand, UX attributes make life better for people like your salesmen and managers because customers are happier with products with a great user experience. Similarly, customers don't care how the job gets done as long as the results are outstanding.

You'll Never Know Who

Unless you are really intimate with a lot of people in your organization, you probably don't really know how all the power flows. That's fine. You don't need to know everyone. It can be tough to be a social butterfly and still get your job done. Besides, if you try too hard you'll get caught up in politics that add no value.

I've been surprised by how things work in some of the places that I've worked. Sometimes accounting and finance have pulled the strings. In other cases, the program managers were the power brokers. In one instance, I ran into an "administrative assistant" who actually made decisions that channeled several hundreds of thousands of dollars per month. She actually had the final word on major sales deals because she performed so many actions on behalf of management.

Because of these uncertainties, I suggest that you always treat everyone as a potential sponge of UX information. Any person could, in turn, spread the message to another person. It is so hard to tell who controls how the nickels and dimes move around.

Many things influence people. It isn't always clear what matters and what does not. The turning point in your UX mission could be a small deed, tiny little action, or the most innocuous email memo. You don't know who and you don't know what will make the difference.

Summary of infiltration tips

- Success is very personal; help others and you'll help yourself.
- Know whether a stakeholder cares about UX methods or UX attributes; adjust your message to best fit.
- It is very difficult to know all stakeholders, especially in an organization; treat everyone fairly and uniformly spread the message of UX.

14

Business Judo: Using Project Momentum to Your Advantage

The time to strike is when the opportunity presents itself.
~ 6th Code of Isshinryu Karate

To me, Judo is like a ballet, except there's no music, no choreography, and the dancers knock each other down.
~ Jack Handy (Saturday Night Live)

Summary

All projects are headed in some direction. You want to understand the vector of activity and inject UX along the way. Catch that rising star. If the project is faltering, you can prevent the fall with the right mix of UX interventions. Businesses worry about failure and you can provide risk mitigation and project insurance. Always look ahead, always be prepared. Have answers to questions the project team didn't even know it had. UX is a project success catalyst and also a failure prevention mechanism for businesses.

The Nature of Opportunity

Opportunity doesn't really knock. There isn't a person walking from cube to cube or office to office banging on doors offering it up. Opportunity is something that you have to recognize. It has many colors, shapes, and sizes.

A failing project can be just as good for you as a project on the path to complete victory. The key is to understand the swing and flow of the project. The greater the changes, the more opportunities you will have. Ups and downs are good things for you. Of course, I like the ups better than the downs.

So, here's your first tip in this chapter. You have to find your own opportunities. You have to make your own magic. This isn't as hard as it sounds. Evaluate your own projects and the other activities around you. Look for changes. Look for issues. Find strengths and weaknesses and prepare to strike.

I'm going to suggest something that I've done for years. You should literally keep a log of projects and opportunities, along with key contacts and UX issues you see along the way. Given my background, I tend to focus on usability issues and information architecture problems but you can focus on other types of UX issues. The trick is documentation and keeping your mind focused on the value you can provide at just the right time.

Actions

Let's get specific. If the project is on the upswing, here's what you do. Find one or two leaders and offer some of your time. All projects need help but often the most successful projects need the most help. This is ironic and counterintuitive but if you think about it, you'll recognize the truth behind it. See the issue, review your documentation, then strike. Offer your help and do what it takes to get your foot in the door.

Once you are on the team, my best advice is to go after the least desirable but highest impact jobs. I've found that assisting with help text and training documentation are good places to hunt. There are many ways to inject UX at this point. For example, you can offer suggestions on language or you can write the text yourself, with just the right nuances.

If you are writing something for the project, you can also start asking a lot of good questions. How many customers have tried this? What were their biggest pain points? How can this be written to help people? All of these kinds of questions can be based on your experience and knowledge of UX.

Here's another key insight. Even if you cannot influence the current project, you will get people thinking that you are a great resource for high impact, undesirable jobs. That builds mojo and goodwill. It also positions you for the next project. You'll be able to inject UX sooner rather than later.

The previous comments apply to both projects on the upswing and downswing. My advice is to find projects that are in flux. You'll be less effective if the project is stagnating. You can't make an impact if the project is sitting still. Move on and find other opportunities. You'll see that there are plenty if you dig around a little.

Positioning and Posturing

As you build goodwill and relationships you will create another opportunity for yourself. You will be able to explain the value of UX in terms that make good sense to project leaders. In particular, you can explain how UX offers protection. That is sweet music to an executive.

On one of my projects for a manufacturing company several years ago I explained that I could increase the chances of project success by 200% or even 300%. Due to my UX knowledge, I said this with self assured confidence. I went on to explain that many projects fail because customers can't figure out how to use products and that training costs often overwhelm help desks. It was simple to provide supporting evidence.

In the UX world, we think about our tools. For example, we talk about usability testing and card sorting. At most we describe what we do and some basic outcomes. The key insight in my little case study above is that I explained the value of UX in extremely simple business terms. I offered the project leader a guarantee. I provided a reasonable measure of risk mitigation and project insurance.

I'm not suggesting that you play on fear and doubt, but business leaders do have concerns about success. You can further augment your position by explaining how you can improve the chances for success, which in turn leads to their personal success.

In all of this activity and in all of these conversations, you need to look ahead several steps. You have the skills to do this. You're a trained thinker. Translate those skills.

Consider for a moment that projects have personalities. They also live, grow and die. Your job is to use what you know. Understand the project and everything that drives it. If you know the project vector and the project personality, you can predict where it is going. That means you can stay ahead of other people. Your UX answers to problems will fall into the right hands at the right time, like magic.

Summary of infiltration tips

- Keep a notebook of UX issues on projects and stay prepared.
- Offer to write help text and documentation, then slip in UX.
- Ask questions that make people think about UX topics.
- Explain how UX offers project insurance and safety.

15

Getting Into the Quality Clubhouse

Every day, buyers like you and I make judgments about quality. But how much of our assessment is due to the actual quality of the item? Not much, I'm afraid. It's not all about quality, but the perception of quality that really counts.
~ Greg Stine

Quality is free. It's not a gift, but it is free. What costs money are the un-quality things—all the actions that involve not doing jobs right the first time
~ Philip Crosby

Summary

Make friends with folks that have anything to do with quality. Learn their lessons and understand their battles. Find ways to piggyback on their activities because you have a lot in common with them. Weasel your way into their hearts and minds, help them succeed, and push them forward. Most corporate drones understand the basics of quality and how it adds value to a project, which provides you with UX knowledge transfer opportunities. While quality teams are not usually rich, they are likely to have bigger budgets than the UX teams. In many circumstances, you can define UX as quality, or as a major contributing factor of quality.

Some Quality Basics

From an idealistic point of view, quality is about making the world a better place. Focusing on a specific domain, such as manufacturing, the definition of quality is significantly more concrete. For example, a quality product would be one that works as intended with a minimum number of problems or failures. This definition treats quality as an attribute but quality should also be considered as a process. It can be a system which ensures proper standards are met, and that products and services meet or exceed customer requirements and expectations.

Quality is much like usability. It can be an attribute or a process. That is, a product can have great usability, or, you can use usability to create a create product. Interestingly, a wonderful user experience is usually a combination of quality and usability. Stated another way, it is difficult to have a great experience if quality if poor. Quality is also like usability in that it is a competitive factor, which can drive success for individuals and organizations.

Because of the similarities between quality and usability there are many lessons which can be transferred. Specifically, quality has a longer and richer history. On the broader subject of user experience, quality also plays an important role, which we'll explore in this chapter.

Where to Find Quality

Quality is in the gut of the customer. While it is sometimes hard to articulate or define, it is usually easy to spot it when it isn't present. Humans have an eye for quality. Then again, perhaps this is a bit idealistic.

Being more realistic, quality is found on the factory floor, in lines of Java code, and in the shopping mall. It is cooked into products and services but it is also an important part of the process that generates those same products and services.

Digging into this, we find that quality is in the minds of the people doing the work. So, it is possible to train people to change what they are doing to improve quality. This is very similar to UX. It isn't something magical and it isn't something that only a few people can do, quite the opposite in fact.

One lesson is that you can find quality manifesting in human resources (HR). They love quality and are willing to invest time, energy, and dollars. Often, senior leaders are involved. But quality activities go beyond HR. There are many organizational manifestations through ISO standards, quality circles, lean teams, and more. Unlike UX, quality is often driven by organization-wide programs and initiatives. Quality has years of backing and thus, years of built-in mindshare. UX specialists can learn from the marketing techniques of the quality folks but also ride on their coattails.

Why Piggyback on Quality Efforts in Your Organization?

It is almost certainly true that more money is being spent on "quality" in your organization than on UX. For many people, especially executives and CEOs, quality translates to money. In several polls, an overwhelming number of top executives indicate that quality contributes to the bottom line, usually through increased revenue from repeat business, customer loyalty, less rework, and general cost savings. Once again, the bottom line is the bottom line. For this reason alone, it is worth getting in bed with the folks involved with quality.

By the way, if you're not completely convinced, keep in mind that quality activities usually reduce customer issue resolution, increase response time, and reduce overall production cycle time. Quality seems to work so there are lessons to learn.

Spend time with people that are working on quality activities. They are engaged in activities that seem to work and senior leaders recognize the rewards. Take a moment to think about UX through the lens of quality. Are there places where you can blend UX and quality? For example, what about UX is repeatable? Can you find ways to reduce variation? How can UX feed sampling and inspection activities?

One path is to simply hijack quality activities and inject UX along the way. Another path is to work with the quality team, explain the value of UX, and get out of the way. Give them UX tools and processes and let them do the work. Let them invade the organization for you, with their money and their time. Still another path is to perform UX activities, get results, and label those activities as quality initiatives. If your goal is to infiltrate, a slight modification to the labels is just fine.

Quality Tools and Intersections with UX

UX professionals have a lot to learn from their quality brethren. For one thing, quality professionals use easy to understand tools, such as scatter diagrams, check sheets, histograms, and Pareto charts. These are also easy to use and explain to others. Card sorting, cognitive walkthroughs and usability testing aren't as straightforward.

Another huge advantage of quality is that it is way more focused on culture change than UX. For example, while Six Sigma, kaizen, and quality circles have an empirical flavor, they are focused on changing organizational processes and employee operations. Naturally, this translates to executive focus and culture change. Senior leaders easily draw a line from these changes to data and metrics, and in turn, the bottom line. Some quality activities even focus everyone on customers' profitability, which is something UX professionals have only begun to consider. In sum, the intrinsic nature of quality drives serious institutionalization, which UX professionals can only dream about.

In all of this, you cannot lose sight of the fact that ultimately people create and maintain quality. Tools, processes, measurements, and metrics are wonderful but only in relation to the humans driving the organization. Like UX, it comes down to people doing great work and making improvements over time. Don't despair; there's definitely room for UX right along with quality. They are siblings.

Summary of infiltration tips

- Quality is an old concept with a lot of mindshare, which means it is worth your time associate UX with quality.
- It is fair to label some UX tools and methods as quality tools and quality methods; hijack where it makes sense.
- Simplify UX to the point where it is as easy to grok as quality, and make it easy for others to explain in case you're not present.
- Take a lesson from the quality playbook: think culture change, like quality, UX is all about how people think and act.

16

Sexy Designs Cloak the Ivory Tower and Dirty Research

Hope is nature's veil for hiding truth's nakedness.
~ Alfred Bernhard Nobel

When they come downstairs from their Ivory Towers,
Idealists are very apt to walk straight into the gutter.
~ Logan Pearsall Smith

Summary

Usability can hide. Great user experience can often built right into products and services but usability never gets recognized because it is hidden in plain sight. Often, the design itself gets credit for ease-of-use. This is because the research done by usability professionals can be effectively buried by designers and developers. Working with the team in this way is an effective infiltration tactic. Keep in mind that most people feel they understand "great design when they see it" and it simply doesn't matter to users and customers where it came from. Getting credit is less important than you might think. Outstanding usability can be equivalent to great design; everyone still wins.

The Value of Camouflage

People who do great work always take pride in their work. Often, this also means taking ownership of the product or service, with the expectation of external recognition and reward.

Unfortunately, doing usability and user experience (UX) work will usually not get you much in the way of accolades. You're more

93

like a ninja – working in the shadows – than a samurai, out on the battlefield. This is especially true if you do UX work inside a large company. You do support work in the eyes of the organization. Your not a general.

But, there's nothing wrong with this. In fact, you can do more good and do more damage working behind other people. You can focus on doing great work versus handling management issues, working through political problems, and working through funding situations.

Don't take your role in the company as a problem. Get your ego out of the picture. You really have an opportunity to focus, focus, focus.

Designers Are Peacocks

When a product is released, the sales team and the marketing organization will often get credit for success. In turn, the design and development team (which you might be part of) will get the second wave of positive feedback.

The sales team will give praise to the product team and the designers, but this is 100% fine. You see, they live and die based on the praise that others lavish on them. They are typically much more creative and extroverted than usability professionals. They need to know that they are needed and loved. If you're ego is out of the way, and you understand your real value to the organization, then usability can slip right in without any mess or any fuss.

It is nearly always in your best interest to stand behind the feathers of the peacocks -- the designers, developers and marketing team. They will promote usability for you, assuming you've done a good job explaining how UX will improve their designers.

That's the key.

You're key job with designers is to show how usability will make their design more sexy. This takes work, but if you do it right, they will carry the torch for you. There will be great loyalty to your current and future inspiration. They don't care that you've done research and that you can produce results. They care about sizzle and sex and flash.

Exploit the situation. Don't try to explain your UX findings or the value of usability research. This is where many usability specialists fall down. You're not selling anything. You're helping feed those people who are experts in selling.

When you understand this difference, you will be warmly welcomed as a key player. It's like supplying exactly the right brush, palette and paint to a great artist. You matter very much, but you're not the peacock.

How to Feed a Peacock

Most usability professionals have a tendency to talk in terms of research. They talk about experiments, research goals, statistical significance, and so forth.

Also, like it or not, the language that we use is not the same that they use. We like to talk about things like ethnographic research, information architecture, personas, and worse. If you look at this from the outside in, it's really nasty.

So, to do this right, you've got to learn their language. You'll find some language is the same no matter where you are. And, you'll even find some overlap with UX (e.g., wireframes). But there's also language that is specific to your organization.

It's more important to understand their language than it is to explain yours. Adapt the language of UX to fit their needs. Create a frame of reference that works for them. Apply your UX empathy skills to making the magic happen.

You don't feed a peacock a baked potato. If you say "heuristic analysis" you're throwing a baked potato at a designer. The peacock won't take a bite.

Do what it takes to learn their language. Discover their pain points and how your data or your research skills can help them succeed. Work to help them succeed which will drive usability into your organization's products and services.

Summary of infiltration tips

- Usability research is often best pushed through designers.
- Learn the jargon of the designers and developers; empathize.
- Avoid the jargon of usability and UX whenever possible.
- Feed designers material that boosts their productivity.
- Read and learn about design; try to walk in their shoes.

17

Artful Intelligence: Mesign, Mevelopment, and Darketing

Sure you can fool some people once or twice, but this is the key lesson of the new marketing: Once fooled, a person will never repeat your story to someone else. If you are not authentic, you will get the benefit of only one sale, not 100.
~ Seth Godin

The aim of marketing is to know and understand the customer so well that the product or service fits him and sells itself.
~ Peter Drucker

Summary

The ideas you have about UX don't mean much if you cannot translate them into something tangible for stakeholders and end customers. Unfortunately, most usability specialists and information architects can't design their way out of a wet paper bag. So, the trick is to become the intelligent link between the creative forces in the organization and the sales and marketing folks. Your explanations of the user experience will gently guide designers in the right direction while simultaneously helping the sales force. You'll be a mentor, translator, and facilitator. If you think of yourself as the pipe between various groups in the organization, you'll quickly realize you can inject a lot of UX influence along the way.

Ask Anyone and You'll Hear "Me"

Most people don't think about other people first. Sure, mothers and fathers think about their children all the time. And, those children come first. But the majority of people out there are necessarily selfish.

In your organization, your fellow workers will talk about their projects and their issues. This is the "me" you'll hear again and again.

Rather than rage against people being self absorbed you can take advantage of the situation. You can turn the proverbial lemons into lemonade.

It seems in most cases that designers, developers and marketers have a strong sense of self. That is, they get very absorbed in their work, their products, their customers, and so on.

There is real value in this "me" focus which you must recognize.

What you should do is be an active listener. This is not obvious advice. You might have tons of great and relevant research, but if you try to preach about it, the me-oriented people will tune you out. But, if you listen to these people closely you will gain friends.

I'm not advocating passive listening. You must be an active listener. You must intentionally focus on who is talking, and you should be able to explain back (i.e., reflect back) what you just heard. Nothing builds a rapport with "me" people better than active listening.

The user experience infiltration tactic here is, once again, quite subtle. You're working hard to understand and influence the people in your organization. Active listening is a key weapon.

These folks will trust you. They will start to listen to your UX advice since they know you care and that you truly understand their art, algorithms, and markets. You'll be one of "them" just by listening and having the right empathy – the same skills you use regularly as a usability professional.

Be Honest: You Aren't a Designer

Many usability professionals claim to be designers. Look, I know that UX people do design and development, but most aren't very good at it at all.

There are some people that are crazy hot and creative. And, they can generate outstanding wireframes and high fidelity prototypes.

But...

We're not designers. We shouldn't pretend to be designers. We're experts at understanding people, observing participants, crunching data, writing standards, and the like.

But we're not designers.

These comments don't apply to everyone, of course. It would be disingenuous to paint with too broad a brush. There obviously are smart, savvy UX designers. There are people who are able to wear 27 hats at once. There are also people who can juggle flaming objects while walking on broken glass, while also reciting Shakespeare.

These people are rare.

Accept your skills. Be brave enough and smart enough to leverage the skills of the people around you.

Designers and developers will respect you if you stick to your knitting, even if they get all the glory. This is where you must put your ego on a shelf.

Yes, understand design and development, but don't take on too much or you'll simply water down your ability to bake usability into your organization over time.

Don't Talk About the Pipe, Be the Pipe

You have unique skills to understand other people. You're in usability and UX and IA because of these skills. Perhaps you even have a degree in sociology or psychology. The point is that you understand people, not just products and services.

Apply these skills for your own benefit and the benefit of your organization. Listen to the designers and developers. Learn how they operate. Study them. Research them, right out in the open.

Next, observe the marketing and sales force. Spend time with them. Lot's and lot's time. Dig in deep and get to the bottom of their concerns and issues.

Now, if you're doing you're job well, you have knowledge and skills to bridge the gap between design, development and marketing. You can get these teams – often quite diverse – to understand each other.

You're going to put on your facilitation hat. As you carry messages between these disparate teams you'll inject your UX knowledge into the mix. You'll possibly inject usability research into the dialogue.

Nothing is more powerful than real data, especially if you can relate it to the work of the "me" people we've looked at in this chapter. And, if you've been actively listening, you're going to be a trusted source. The data will go down like a glass of tall, cool water on a hot summer day.

Summary of infiltration tips

- Many people are "me" focused; recognize this to succeed.
- Position yourself according to the needs of other people.
- Actively listen to win the hearts and minds of the "me" people.
- From your position of trust, be the pipeline and inject UX.

18

The Old Switcheroo:
Delivering Answers and Solutions

We will go into your houses and redesign them the same way your web sites are designed. The basement will be the first thing you see, the kitchen will be unreachable except through the bedroom and both bathrooms, the bedroom will be on six different floors, and the dog will be in every room at once.

~ Ann Feeny

He must be very ignorant for he answers every question he is asked.

~ Voltaire

Summary

Do not talk about methods, activities, or functionality. In other words, don't talk about the path, talk about the end result. You'll be tempted, but don't talk about processes or policies either. These things are necessary for business to transpire but they are not needed to sell UX. Instead, it is always key to focus on answers and solutions; the things that matter to the business at hand. The outcomes and benefits to customers and the business are far more important than any research you have done or any data that you've collected over time.

Are We Too Smart for Our Own Good?

I think we have a problem: We have too much education. We have too much knowledge. We understand customers too well. Quite honestly, I think we are too smart for our own good.

Here's the problem...

We are seen as talking down from the Ivory Tower, with big ideas. Although we all care about people, we are seen as being too

105

conceptual and lofty. We know that UX'ers are a practical bunch of folks but we don't sound that way to other people.

I'm sure that you've faced situations where you're trying to explain a particular testing situation. Or, maybe you're explaining a special technique to a project manager or developer. The person listening to you probably doesn't care too much. I know this sounds a bit harsh but a good splash of cold water in the face never hurt anyone.

In Business, It's the Results that Matter

You should not take offense when someone isn't listening to you about heuristic analysis, ethnographic research, or a pluralistic walkthrough. Remember, this is your jargon. It doesn't actually represent the value that you offer to your organization.

That's right, I'm saying that the tools don't matter. What really matter are the results. This is precisely the reason why you shouldn't take offense when someone outside UX glazes over at what you're saying about your toolbox. If they drool on the floor take that as a hint that you're getting too technical on them. You're using jargon that isn't helping them understand the results and the bottom line benefits.

What it does mean is that you have to change the way that you think about your skills, methods and techniques. Here's an analogy. It doesn't matter that there's a CPU, RAM, and a fan inside your computer. I mean, sure, the engineering is elegant but you probably don't care too much. Instead, you care that you can turn it on, click the mouse, type on the keyboard, and get your job done. In fact, what really matters is that you're able to type a letter to Grandma in Microsoft Word, and that you're able to print it out or email it. The results matter, not what's happening in the guts of your machine.

When to Talk About "Boring" Stuff

There are three times when I advise you to talk about UX methods. Keep in mind that most people aren't interested in our jargon or language. It is difficult to follow along, much the same way you're probably confused when a nuclear physicist is talking to you.

We throw around many more crazy words than you might realize.

So, here are the three places where it makes sense to talk about UX using our jargon. Let's look at each one at a time:

First, if someone is writing up a contract, creating official artifacts, or otherwise generating legal paperwork, then I recommend using UX jargon. More importantly, you'll want to be very specific about the tools and techniques using the appropriate language.

It's critical that you provide a few sentences that clearly explain the expected outcome. This is really something you don't want to miss.

The reason that I recommend talking about UX in this situation is that you'll be able to legally require or "lock in" a specific UX technique or method. If anyone questions the approach, you'll have it in writing. I'm not saying be devious about this. I'm saying that you want to make sure that you've got the requirements locked down and the solution defined for anyone to see.

Second, you definitely should use the language of UX when you are talking to people that understand and want to use that language. In most cases this will mean that you are talking to your peers. Those peers might be in your organization or maybe not. Perhaps you're part of an organization, forum or membership online. In that case, consider yourself in a safe zone.

Third, I strongly recommend that you use UX language if a product manager or executive makes a direct request. If they want to know exactly what you did, first explain the outcome and benefits. Don't start with UX language. However, if they press and want to really know what you did then explain it. After you've explained the benefits and the process then you're free to talk about UX using UX jargon. If you're getting blank expressions then drop it like a hot coal.

Why It's Important to Translate Features Into Benefits

The advice in this chapter is that you should be aware of what you're saying in reference to your UX actions. Rather than try to explain how you get the work done using jargon take a step back and think about how your work is really delivering bottom line value.

Smart engineers and developers are the ones who are able to create elegant solutions. Valuable engineers are the ones who can solve problems in relation to the bottom line. But really, the top 1% of engineers and developers create elegant solutions for the organization, boost profits, but also explain what they've done in plain language.

As a usability professional or UX guru, you're job is to solve problems for the company. Your job is to use your skills and techniques to help the organization deliver value to customers. And as you're making the magic happen you want to use language that virtually anyone can understand. If you do this, your job will be secure. You'll advance in the company. You'll get funding and you'll grow professionally.

Summary of infiltration tips

- Don't let intelligence get in the way of simple communication.
- People care about the results you offer, not your jargon.
- There are three time where jargon is OK to use; be careful.
- Brilliant success is the result of an elegant UX solution which has a net positive impact on the bottom line, which you can explain in language that any 8th grade student could easily grasp.

19

Match Your Activity to the Culture of Victory

*It is better to lead from behind and to put others in front,
especially when you celebrate victory when nice things occur.
You take the front line when there is danger. Then people
will appreciate your leadership.*
~ Nelson Mandela

Victory has a thousand fathers, but defeat is an orphan.
~ John F. Kennedy

Summary

Do not get wrapped around the axle of any particular UX technique. Adapt to the needs of the company and, importantly, the culture of success. Understand which projects have been successful and learn their tricks and techniques. Get to know the people that were involved and what they did to win. Once you have done this research and networking, adjust your UX toolbox to match. Find the gaps where usability, interaction design, and information architecture will add value. My advice is to avoid dog programs. It is better to find the shining stars. Tag along and emulate the success.

Find the Nuggets of Gold

Every company has success stories. Your job is to unearth these success stories, understand them through and through, and then hijack them for your own purposes. The idea is to marry up user experience tactics and techniques with these successful projects. It isn't too hard figure out how the user experience was part of the victory.

111

In a sense, you're going to be a parasite on projects that have already achieved a level of success. You'll adopt these projects as your own by making people understand how the user experience had an impact. You won't take credit for the projects of course, but you will focus the lens of user experience on the projects.

The Secret of the Parasite

Here's exactly what you're going to do. First, you're going to ask everyone around you to name two or three projects that have done fantastic. Or, perhaps you'll ask about products or services that customers rave about. The first idea, in other words, is to make sure you know what people in your organization value.

Second, you're going to document these projects. In writing, you're going to outline what happened, when it happened, and who was involved. History belongs to the person who writes it. Wink, wink.

Third, you're going to verify that what you've documented is accurate. Again, you're not trying to steal or otherwise claim that these projects, products, or services that have been successful are your own. You're like a reporter trying to get the story straight. Documentation is absolutely essential; don't skip this step.

Fourth, you're going to follow-up with the top two or three people involved directly in the project. You're going to get even more details. You're going to dig in and get the story straight. You're also going to ask some leading questions. What I'm saying is that you'll ask questions that relate to usability and user experience. I can guarantee that these things are part of the success, even though no one has previously talked about it.

Believe it or not, at this point you've built a case study. You can convert this case study into a white paper, internal report, or an executive summary for project leaders, your team, or other people that you want to influence.

Yes, you've hijacked a project. But, not in a bad way. Instead, what you've done is simply found a way to inject usability into organization documents. And all you needed to do was get people talking and write down what they've said. Of course, you did have to ask some questions to get people to think about usability and user experience. But don't you think that's a small price to pay?

Building Bridges

As part of your success story investigation, you should also try to capture as much of the corporate or organization jargon as you can. Absolutely adopt this as your own.

Just as you're injecting user experience language into your case studies, you're going to inject your organizations jargon into your usability documentation and reports. The idea it is to better align your work with the work of the organization. This synchronization is extremely powerful and gets everyone seeing eye to eye, and using the same language in no time.

You can also use this approach when you're trying to figure out what you ought to call your techniques and methods. In other words, rather than saying heuristic analysis, you might say expert review. The reason you do this is because other people in your organization are calling your heuristic analysis an expert review.

You really shouldn't care about labels. The end result is the same after all. That is, the technique doesn't change, just the label. How simple is that? And, it's painless too. Everyone wins.

I'll make a point here about flexibility and adaptability. You really don't need to take pride in the name of a technique. However, you do need to care about utilizing the technique or method at the right time, and generating bottom-line results that people understand. Know where to draw the line and you'll be far more successful than you can imagine.

Dogs and Stars

All companies have star projects and dog projects. The star projects are the ones that get the money and attention. These are the ones that really mean something to the organization. The dog projects are the ones that no one wants to be on, are poorly funded, and won't impact the bottom line. It's true that some star projects can fade and that some dog projects can turn around, but that doesn't happen too often. Once there's momentum the stars take off and the dogs languish. I've seen this hundreds of times and I'll bet you have too.

I'm going to give you advice that might seem counterintuitive. Usability professionals have a strong tendency and desire to fix what's broken. It's true; think about it. As a result, we tend to work on losing projects. That hurts.

The dog projects get beaten into the ground. And get a load of this. User experience gets a bad name because we've made bad choices about what were going to work on. Did you ever consider that before? The projects you choose can help or hurt the usability cause.

The raw truth is that when you have the choice, you must avoid the dog projects and run with the stars. You must try to work with the stronger teams, embrace the funding, and accept the accolades when the entire team succeeds. This is instrumental to your long term value.

Here's a caveat...

If a project is really in the dumps due to usability problems then by all means jump on board and wave your magic wand. However, it is very rare for a project to merely have problems that are related to the user experience.

Most likely, the project is not well-funded, the customer doesn't want what you're selling, the technology is old, senior executives don't care about it, or something else that simply has nothing at all to do with usability. Therefore, there ain't nothing you can do about it. Avoid those dogs like the plague.

Jump on the success train. Take it for a ride.

Summary of infiltration tips

- Control history through documentation and story telling.
- Labels don't really matter so just use what people give you.
- As a rule, it's best to avoid projects that are going to flame out.
- Embrace the success stories in your organization; find the UX messages embedded in those projects.

20

Win by Losing in a Sea of Egos, Politics and Smelly Shoes

A good listener tries to understand what the other person is saying.
In the end he may disagree sharply, but because he disagrees,
he wants to know exactly what it is he is disagreeing with.
~ Kenneth A. Wells

Hard conditions of life are indispensable to bringing out the best
in human personality.
~ Alexis Carrel

Summary

Sometimes it makes good sense to just give up. There are many places where you can make solid progress, so if you feel you are in an uphill battle, look for more fertile grounds. There are also times where you will be caught in a political firestorm. Be aware of this possibility and when you have doubts, fall back on data, metrics, benchmarks, and research. Take a calculated look at the situation and remain as passionless as possible if the political landscape gets too hot. People will appreciate and remember your even keel and smart responses. Build up the mojo which in turn can be used to barter UX.

To Debate Or Not, That is the Question

In my experience, user experience professionals and usability specialists like to debate. They like to talk. They like to jump into conversations and figure things out. We're curious bunch, don't you agree?

However, this way of interacting with other people is sometimes academic and not practical whatsoever. Some people will claim that they have superior knowledge of the customer. For example, I've seen this when UX'ers and folks from sales and marketing all get together. You'll see explosions when there are opinions floating around from this motley crew.

My advice in most cases is to roll over. The reason is that sales and marketing folks really do have valuable opinions. Your job isn't to prove they are wrong but to use the information they're sharing with you. It's solid gold.

What If There Is the Need for a Fight?

If you're doing battle with other folks in your organization then you need to be prepared. You've gotta be loaded for bear, as my grandfather always liked to say.

What this means is that you have to check your opinions at the door. What you need are facts. You need cold hard data to back up what you're saying.

And, if you don't have data?

Well, then you need to clearly explain your plan to gather data. You'll want to explain how to do it fast and cheap. You want to demonstrate the return on investment for this data too. If you can tell a story or provide a case study where the data made a huge difference, you'll be at a major advantage.

Why Is There a Fight?

Before you dig your heels in, I strongly suggest that you reflect on what is causing the fight to occur. Is an executive pushing for change? Is the product team unhappy? Is the market changing and there's fear in the air? Find the root of the disturbance and focus on the solution.

Furthermore, there's no reason to get personal or attack an individual. What you're trying to do is understand the real issue. Obviously if you're involved then UX is part of the problem, solution, or both.

Dig into the questions flying around. Know the situation and you'll be a mile ahead when the discussion really gets going.

The Final Answer

When it comes down to it you really only have two masters to service. First, you have to ensure that you're meeting the business objectives set forth by the organizational leaders. Very likely the objectives will be tied to the bottom line. Second, you must ensure that the customers are being properly represented.

I strongly encourage you to map all of your UX activity back to the goals of your business. If you can show this relationship again and again you will win friends and influence people. Trust me on that.

Now, regarding your customers here's a little trick that I like to use. I gather up as much data as I can from around the organization as it relates to customers. You have to really think about what this means because some data is hard to find. It's subtle too, and often hidden in the nooks and crannies of a business.

Once you've gathered up this data then you'll want to map that data to the data you've collected. That is, you'll draw parallels and relations between all the data you have – including the UX data that you've extracted over the years.

You're looking for commonality so that you can tell a great story to people when a fight erupts. By the way, this "fight" might simply be an executive presentation that you're giving. My point is that it's very hard to argue with data.

Now comes the knockout punch. Because you know the goals of the business, and because you have an outstanding cross section of metrics, and because you have strong stories, you'll be nearly unbeatable.

You won't need to justify anything to anyone. You'll simply present the facts, tell the story, and provide the strong UX solution. Unless people are 100% emotionally driven in the "fight" you'll come out ahead because you've used a strong dose of common sense with a heavy helping of data. Jab, jab, jab, uppercut!

While you might have data that suggests one particular facet of the answer, keep in mind that they might have data too. So, if you do decide to debate, bring data to the fight.

Your Personality Can Work for You or Against You

Some people have the tendency to throw all of their passion at a problem. While conviction can drive persuasion it can also cloud judgment and turn people off. If you are a "hot head" or if you let your emotions get the best of you, consider moderating your comments about UX using the two techniques below.

First, you can prepare ahead of time. You can rehearse what you're going to say and how you're going to say it. If you can prepare I encourage you to do so. Words are your friend. Furthermore, I very strongly recommend that you write down what you are thinking. Put your thoughts down in the context of any data you've been able to acquire as I've discussed previously.

Second, don't talk to people; listen to them. If you feel the battle is starting to heat up and you haven't prepared or documented anything, then be a pacifist. That is, actively listen to what the other person is saying. This is true even when your position or ideas are being attacked. Remain calm and listen. If you have a hard time listening then ask questions and take notes. This works like a charm. It's hard to talk and write at the same time.

By the way, let me make a Captain Obvious comment: Being courteous is absolutely the way to go. People like to do business with calm, easy going people. While being aggressive is sometimes needed, as a general rule taking the Zen path will lead to inner and outer peacefulness. And interestingly, this is the path of greater understanding and wealth.

I like to think about these actions as building up good karma or mojo. You'll be amazed at how much people listen to you when they know you have a level head. There's an unwritten rule that the person who listens the best has the most important thing to say. If that's not a quote, then please go ahead and quote me. Hang it up on the wall and mediate on it for good measure.

Summary of infiltration tips

- Instead of fighting to be right, actively listen to what the organization is really trying to tell you about UX.
- Gather data, analyze it, combine it with your own data so that you're prepared for anything; develop stories and case studies.
- Keep your personality in check if you're prone to argumentation or if your ego gets in the way; ask questions and document the answers that people are giving to you.

21

Jargon, Part One: Talk Simple

We are searching for some kind of harmony between two intangibles: a form which we have not yet designed and a context which we cannot properly describe.
~ Christopher Alexander

Our business is infested with idiots who try to impress by using pretentious jargon.
~ David Ogilvy

Summary

It is imperative to simplify your language in discussions about user experience with people who aren't familiar with it. Like it or not, UX isn't the easiest concept to grasp and the research techniques take a little time to explain. Many people equate UX with quality, design, or market research. Don't let this bother you but instead find ways to use these conceptions to your advantage. Use some judo! Draw parallels and use analogies, all while using unambiguous language. Similarly, consider developing slogans and buzz points you can use over and over. An elevator speech is essential to your success.

Sophistication Always Sinks the Ship

I often find myself giving advice to people writing documents. It's not that I'm a stickler for details, or even a great writer. Instead, it's my passion for the user experience. In reference to writing, I'm talking about the helping readers. I literally picture myself in the reader's shoes, with the book, article or document in my hands, scanning word by word and going through sentence by sentence. I find myself asking questions such as, "Does this make any sense at all? Do I get it?"

I'm sure you've run into this yourself when you're reading something unfamiliar. Aren't you frustrated by acronyms when you see them for the first time and they have not been defined?

At least once a week someone asks me what UX is. So, I am constantly defining it right up front. You should try to do the same. Instead of writing UX try writing user experience (UX) the first time. After that, write UX all you want.

The Key is to Provide Context

If you find it absolutely necessary to talk about usability then please take the time up front to define exactly what you're talking about. Be precise. Explain everything in clear language; there's no point in trying to be sophisticated or to inject complications. If you use complicated language you'll just seem aloof, like an Ivory Tower academic out of touch with business reality.

Product managers, executives, programmers, developers, and many other people will understand what you're talking about once it's been explained. The trick is to provide a framework. That is, you must provide context. Give them the background and they'll follow right along without any problems.

In the same way that an astrophysicist talking about how black holes are created would confuse you, the people in your organization will be easily confused if you don't start off on the right foot. Again, there's no point in dazzling these folks. You're trying to win them over. You're trying to integrate usability into the organization and to do that you need their acceptance. Your language is a key to success.

Usability Means Quality, Design, and Marketing

You'll find that most people who are unfamiliar with usability and the concepts of user experience will make a leap to what they already understand. For example, some people think that usability is the same thing as quality. Still others think that usability is entirely related to design, or marketing.

You can't blame people for thinking this way. People learn new concepts and ideas based on their current knowledge base and understanding of the world. Furthermore, as we all know, it takes time and effort to learn and integrate new ideas. We're all comparison machines – how's this new thing like that old thing I understand?

This is why I very strongly encourage you to provide background and context. Simplify the literal words, phrases and sentences that you use. You're not dumbing anything down by doing this. You're just making it easier for other people to understand exactly what you're talking about.

Here's another trick. Instead of allowing people to create their own analogies, why not create analogies for them? I find it very helpful to use stories and case studies to make it clear what I'm talking about. It's not hard to jump from a story or a case study to an analogy that really makes sense. This is one way that I separate usability from quality, design, and marketing.

If there is resistance to what you're saying there is still another tactic you can use. Simply accept that people equate usability to something else in the organization. That's fine. What you'll do is blend usability into their frameworks. This is the opposite of trying to separate them cleanly. In a sense, you're being a "parasite" in a manner that I described in the previous chapter.

Slogans and Buzz

In some organizations you might really get traction with this technique. We're talking about language and communication and with that in mind, you might want to come up with a very simple slogan that people understand and relate to your usability efforts.

You don't want anything tacky or otherwise glitzy. You don't want to go over the top and you're not going to create a jingle. But, you do want to borrow the methods and techniques that marketers have used for more than 60 years. You're trying to create a mental shortcut for people.

Come up with a phrase that is short and simple. It should clearly summarize what you or your team offers to the organization. Since every business is unique you'll probably have to spend a little time thinking this one through for yourself. But, eventually you will find something that clearly summarizes your value to the organization. Once you have this phrase or sentence, you want to start including it in your paperwork. Furthermore, you can edit your signature and e-mails. You can add it to your own section of the intranet. Inject that slogan everywhere.

The bottom line is to get the word out there. Promote a little bit. No one's going to mind. Welcome to Branding 101.

The Power of the Elevator Speech

Most user experience professionals have been caught off guard at one time or another. Maybe it was an executive asking a question about some research being performed. Or, may be was a product manager or developer who's trying to figure out what goes on in the usability lab. The bottom line is that you're bound to be surprised at some point. Yes, it happens to all of us.

Being caught off guard is never fun. The antidote is preparation. By knowing exactly who you are and what you do, you'll be more prepared to answer any questions thrown your way. Unfortunately, most people really don't know what they do or the value they provide to the organization. You must understand the needs of the business and how you add to the bottom line, all for the sake of the user of course. Know exactly why you're valuable.

Let's talk more about being prepared. I'm going to throw an idea at you that isn't new. This is something that I'm sure you've heard of before. The idea is the elevator speech. The concept is very easy to grasp. Imagine that you only have 30 seconds to explain exactly what you do, who you are, and the value you provide. Imagine further that you're stuck in an elevator with the CEO of your company, and he's asking you tough questions. Now imagine successfully answering all of those questions. In this situation, preparation is essential.

This is a tried-and-true technique that smart job applicants certainly understand. What you're doing is summarizing for the sake of clarity. Brevity is essential. You're cutting to the heart of the matter.

By mastering the elevator speech it'll be virtually impossible to be caught off guard when you're asked a question about usability. In fact, you'll have the upper hand. You'll know what you do, how you fit in the organization, and your bottom line impact. You'll stun them!

When you're developing your Elevator Speech, remember, don't use jargon. Don't focus on your techniques and methods. Don't try to justify the work you do. Keep it simple, keep it clean. Answer the questions that matter and demonstrate that you provide business value in no uncertain terms.

Summary of infiltration tips

- Define an acronym the first time you use it.
- Provide context; give people the background.
- Leverage stories and case studies; create easy analogies.
- Construct a compelling and high value elevator speech; use it.

22

Jargon, Part Two: Use Their Language, Steal Their Thoughts

It is one of the most beautiful compensations of this life that no man can sincerely try to help another without helping himself.
~ Ralph Waldo Emerson

I think there should be something in science called the "reindeer effect." I don't know what it would be, but I think it'd be good to hear someone say, "Gentlemen, what we have here is a terrifying example of the reindeer effect."
~ Jack Handy

Summary

Learn the language. Some companies call tasks action items whereas others call tasks to dos. Tie the language of UX to the language of the company. Better still, slowly but surely inject UX language into documents and emails. Repeat, repeat, repeat. It will take time but if you control the language, you control the concepts. So, avoid most UX jargon but do what you can inject it where it makes sense. Consider piggybacking on language already used that lines up with user experience.

Every Company Has Its Own Secret Handshake

For some reason, businesses feel a need to create their own language. They create words out of thin air that don't mean anything to an outsider. For example, in one company that I worked for, tasks were called action items. Yet in another company that I work for, the tasks were called to dos. They are exactly the same: stuff that's got to get done.

I'm sure that your organization is no different. You have your own language. It's like a Law of Dilbert: "Thou Shall Use Jargon!" Rather than fight this, use it to your advantage. In just a moment I'll talk about this in great detail. In fact, I'm going to give you a secret for injecting user experience language into your organization. It's slick! But first, I want to talk about simply using the words available to you.

You'll want to adopt the language everyone else is using. This is more significant than you might realize. You're going to make sure that you use the jargon that everyone else in your organization uses. This drives up your credibility and shows to everyone else that you're an insider; you know, one of them. Of course, don't use jargon just for the sake of jargon. Use it where it makes sense.

What's this mean in context? How can you take action? That's simple. I've seen many sterile reports written by usability professionals. It takes very little to convert these reports into very readable, even fun reports. The trick is to add common language. Use the language of the organization, especially if the content is staying internal. Use their acronyms and sayings.

But there's more…

Use stories, customer testimonials, and the like, in your reports. This injects humanity into your reports. That's a real secret. In the same way that short clips of customers interacting with a product during a usability test can impress product managers and CEOs, testimonials and case studies really grab attention and pack a punch.

This tactic works because it's so visceral. It's easy to understand and grasp that a customer doesn't like something about your widget. They explain what doesn't work. They pave the way. All you need to do is capture that story and use it when appropriate.

Here's something else to ponder. Jargon and acronyms are meant to simplify. They are shortcuts. But ironically, they confuse people, especially those folks that are new to an organization. However, stories and case studies take up a lot of room. They also take time.

They provide overwhelming value to an organization. They must be added to your user experience infiltration tactics toolbox.

From Egg to Pupa to Larva to Butterfly

Here's something that is a bit sneaky. I love doing this. First, you volunteer to be the notetaker. You're the one who takes meeting minutes. You're the one who crafts the reports. By doing this, you control the words, language and even new jargon that is created. It isn't too hard as you're writing to inject the language of usability.

In addition you'll want to volunteer to give presentations. You'll pull in testimonials and case studies, you'll use the language of your customers, but also the language of usability. You're educating people but you're also dominating the future. Others will start borrowing words and phrases from you. You'll be the master of the jargon.

What you're doing is injecting the customer into your documentation. By doing this you take control. You are literally shaping how your company thinks about customers.

You're much more than a scribe. You are the leader who understands how customers think, and quite literally you become an authority. It all starts by simply volunteering to take some notes. This is such a great guerilla tactic, don't you think?

Lend a Helping Hand

Here's a similar tactic. Obviously you can't write everything but you can certainly volunteer to proofread. Many people writing reports are looking for help. So, create an opportunity. Ask to help. Offer proof reading services.

Of course what you'll do is find ways to inject usability into the document. It isn't too hard to suggest case studies and testimonials that come directly from customers.

All of this assumes that you've been keeping good records. If you aren't keeping rock solid records I strongly encourage you to start immediately. In terms of infiltration tactics, this is imperative. You must have raw material to work with. And, absolutely think beyond data that you get directly, hands-on in the lab. Be sure to find user experience anecdotes throughout the organization. Become a familiar face; get people to talk, listen, and take notes.

By the way, a related tactic is to give people samples of work that you've generated in the past. Give them documents that you've written that include testimonials and usability data that are clear and obvious. Encourage them to use your framework and to borrow heavily on what you've crafted. Let them inject usability for you.

Language is Behind Every Sale

You definitely want to think beyond jargon as you're reading this chapter. You're learning real marketing tactics. You're learning to line up your skills to the needs of customers and ultimately the bottom line. You're doing it by controlling language. You're doing it by controlling documentation and shaping how people think within your company, and about your organization.

You should never be ashamed of marketing. Remember, your objective as a usability specialist goes far beyond conducting research and generating recommendations. You have an obligation to your organization's bottom line and your customers. The only way to achieve overwhelming victory is to be strong. You're marketing for the sake of your customers!

I know many marketers; I've read hundreds of articles, and dozens of books on marketing. I have a strong business background and one thing is blatantly clear: language is the number one marketing weapon on the planet. It doesn't matter if you're talking about the spoken word or the written word, language is behind every sale. Use it wisely.

Summary of infiltration tips

- Use words that make sense in context; use jargon sparingly.
- Stories and testimonials are always better than jargon.
- Volunteer to write and edit; you'll soon be an info juggernaut.
- You can easily do "soft sell" marketing by controlling jargon.

23

The Power of Your Email Signature

*You're probably sending e-mail because you're deep
in thought about something. Your reader is too,
only they're deep in thought about something else.*
~ Steve Robbins

I have no life, just e-mail.
~ Michael Jantze, The Norm (Daily Comic Strip)

Summary

You can make a simple update to your outgoing email that will result in hundreds or even thousands of UX advertisements for free every year. The idea is to include a link, quote, or idea related to UX in your email signature. You're looking for something to attract attention and generate interest. Experiment until you find something that causes people to take action. Maybe they'll click on a link, maybe they'll respond to your email with a note, or maybe they'll stop you in the hall to talk about UX. Skip to the end of the chapter now if you're looking for some examples.

Return on Investment

If you are like 98% of the other people online, you spend a huge fraction of your time reading and writing email. Some people, like me, send fifty or more emails every day. Every email going out is an opportunity to spread the ideas of user experience.

Let's work the odds. If you send out 30 emails per day on average, you'll be sending out over 1,000 emails per year. If your response rate is only 1%, you'll have 10 people take action per year. In this example, that's about one response per month. Not too shabby.

Hopefully this convinces you to make the investment in a good signature. For the most part, this is a one time investment. Set up your signature in your email client and forget about it. The marketing effort after that initial set up is zip, zilch, zero. Create and forget.

By the way, the little example above doesn't even take forwarded emails into consideration, nor does it reflect email replies. I've seen some email trails that include 5, 10, or even 15 responses. That means that your message is spreading around.

Viral Marketing Benefits

Even when people don't take action based on your signature, you are still distributing your message. While your main intention is to get other people to take action, you can still spread the UX message and gain mindshare. People will see your signature and learn that you care about user experience. If they know this, you will be a lightening rod when UX comes up in conversations. People will seek you out.

I have also seen something else that is interesting. Other people use my UX quotes in their own email messages. This makes the message viral. It spreads without any effort once others have picked it up.

Along a similar vein, I've had people ask me for more information about quotes that I've used. These folks want to know more so that they can use the information in their presentations or papers. This is more likely to happen if you focus on the business benefits of UX, such as return on investment or risk mitigation.

People like snappy and insightful quotes but they also have interest in web sites and books. I've pointed to great articles and I've pointed to great books. I've included all kinds of material in my signature and so can you.

General Advice

If you like this UX infiltration tactic, my strongest advice is to experiment. I won't tell you to constantly change your signature but I will stress the importance of trying new approaches until you find an effective approach.

If you want to create a signature that has some buzz you'll need to treat your signature as if it is an advertisement. Along these lines, if you don't know anything about copywriting now is a good time to learn. It is a great skill to have and it'll also get you thinking more about marketing. Your overall writing will get better too.

I advise you to pass your signature by a few people before you take it prime time. Do some quick testing if you aren't clear if something is going to work or not. This will improve your chances of success. Also, you'll probably need to do a lot less experimentation to create a smash hit signature.

If you work in a large company you might be restricted in what you can add to your emails, so be careful. I haven't heard of anyone getting in trouble because they added interesting, useful, and helpful UX material to their email signatures but hey, you never know.

My last bit of advice is a real bonus. This is actually much more effective than adding UX material to your email signature. The next time you update your voice mail message, add something jazzy about user experience. Add an interesting quote or statistic to your message. When people call you, they get a little UX advertisement. Keep it short and sweet, but definitely give this a try. I do strongly advise making frequent updates. Voice mail messages get attention. They work.

Three Examples That Have Worked

The examples below have been winners for me in the past. I've modified them just a bit for a few reasons, but they are close enough to get your juices flowing.

= = = = = = = = = = = = = = = = = = = =
John S. Rhodes
Email: john@webword.com
Cell: 555-555-1212
Web: http://webword.com

328% Return on Investment? Absolutely, completely, totally, YES!
http://webword.com

= = = = = = = = = = = = = = = = = = = =
John S. Rhodes
Email: john@webword.com
Phone: 555-555-1212
Web: http://webword.com

User interface is 47% - 60% of the lines of system or application code.
~ Macintyre, Estep and Sieburth

= = = = = = = = = = = = = = = = = = = =
John S. Rhodes
Email: john@webword.com
Cell: 555-555-1212

Are your customers angry that your web site doesn't work?
Get answers!
http://webword.com

Summary of infiltration tips

- Treat your email signature like it is an advertisement.
- Your email signature should include UX tips, advice, and links.
- You won't get it right the first time so you must experiment.
- Bonus: update your voice mail message with UX information.

24

Make It Personal, Make It Physical

The great gift of human beings is that we have the power of empathy.
~ Meryl Streep

If you care passionately about usability and accessibility, and you want your organization's Web site to be usable, you will have to convince people it's important. People who don't think about usability aren't going to suddenly start thinking about it because the boss sends out a memo. So make the case for usability. It starts with you.
~ Chris McEvoy

Summary

Baby steps. The best way to educate people on UX is to demonstrate its value on something very specific and personal. Find the time to work face to face with the folks that matter on your projects. Talk about the great design of a coffee cup handle. Explain how the DVD player is so hard to use. It is best to have your ears open when other folks talk and look for usability issues, then strike. The caveat is that you must stay positive. Don't allow people to think about UX in negative terms. There's a fine line between an insightful UX conversation and a cesspool of complaints.

You've Got Empathy, So Use It

Usability professionals have incredible empathy. As a rule, they're able to really feel and understand what other people are thinking and experiencing. They're willing to walk a mile in someone else's shoes. It's incredible really, and it's a reason why I love usability specialists.

So what boggles my mind is that in a corporate environment these same usability professionals neglect to utilize the skills for their advantage. They don't use these skills for their own benefit or really even the benefit of the organization to the maximum degree.

It's frustrating!

I'm specifically talking about usability professionals spending time to really get to know their coworkers for the sake of improving the bottom line. Certainly these people are courteous and they care about others in the workplace but they don't consider their actions, and their ability to empathize so well, as a means of achieving the goals of the organization. This is such an easy win.

I very strongly recommend that you get to know the people around you for the sake of improving your position in the company and to carry the banner of usability. You'll want to get to know the pain that people are feeling in the workplace. These pain points are opportunities for you to help. You're good at helping others and you know it. Grab the ball and run.

You need to know more about your coworkers' biases, decision-making skills, mannerisms, and everything else. These are the same things that you might observe in a research study.

In essence, you're treating your coworkers as users – your customers, actually. This is an incredibly powerful tip that will help you position yourself as a trusted resource. Ready, willing, and able to help others achieve success. Gather that data!

Empathy and altruism will take you a long way in the corporate environment. People are looking for meaning in a soulless company and you can provide it. They're looking for people who are well rounded and who have genuine concern for their needs. Usability professionals are uniquely positioned to capitalize on their skills. Are you following me?

How You Communicate: Face-to-Face is the Clear Winner

In addition to having the right mindset and applying empathy in the right place and the right time, there are certain ways of operating that will also take you a long way. I'm talking about how you literally conduct business on a day-to-day basis. I'm talking directly about how you communicate and interact with your coworkers.

It's difficult to really exploit your empathetic skills if you're using electronic communication asynchronously. To put it simply, when you use e-mail you can't read and understand the feelings and emotions of the person on the other end. When they email you back you're likewise blinded. You're an innocent little kitten in most cases. For this reason, I strongly recommend that you choose face-to-face communications with your coworkers whenever possible.

Let's explore this. Consider the email interactions you've had with other people. What's worked? Why hasn't? Have you ever had a problem with coworker due to an email misunderstanding? Even people who are intelligent and well spoken eventually run into problems due to email and its facelessness. Again, it's hard to have empathy in its truest sense without more personal communications.

Obviously it makes sense to use email in many situations. But if you're trying to extract biases and subtle nuances, face-to-face is key. So, set up in-person meetings, visit someone in their cubicle, take them to lunch, and be in the physical presence of that person.

In the sales world this is called pressing the flesh. That sounds sinister but it just means that you need human contact to win big sales. Relationships on names and faces, not emails.

Still not convinced?

Think of the power of a handshake. Think about the power and importance of eye contact. If you wish to bring usability into an organization you need to be a strong player and that means you need marketing skills. Empathize and stay in touch with people to become a true champion of usability.

As a tangent, the most well-rounded and likable people I know are the ones who spend time with me face-to-face. They are approachable. I feel comfortable just spending time with them. They listen well and they are genuine. You can bet your bottom dollar that they choose face-to-face conversations above all others; it becomes reciprocal.

In short, they choose to press the flesh. So should you.

The Ethnographic Sneak Attack

Here is a sneak attack that I love. What you do is simply observe people in their natural environment. For example, just watch them use their computer. Just watch them use the phone in their office. In very little time you'll see that they get frustrated with some aspect of their tools. Technology will fail them and you'll be looking for it.

Next, what you'll do is make some friendly conversation about this frustration. You'll dig into that. In a sense, you're doing an ethnographic study on your coworker. You're gathering data on what works and doesn't work for them.

Now it's time to strike. You'll empathize with them. You'll share their frustrations. This is your opportunity to talk about usability in the real world. For example, talk about DVD players, cars, appliances, iPods, and other familiar technology. Talk about what works and doesn't work. Really try to have a fun conversation. Play around.

You probably know what's coming next. At this point you can start talking about usability and user experience in the context of your business. You can talk about how your customers are probably frustrated with your organization's products. You might even have some evidence of this, such as an anecdote or maybe even direct data that you've gathered.

This is such a simple way to get people to understand the value you provide. Just showing you understand their pain goes a long way in creating and growing credibility. It's also a powerful hook to start a meaningful usability conversation.

Physical, Like Raw Meat on a Hook

The most important person in the entire organization is the one you're talking to. People like to talk about themselves, their families, and their situations. They think selfishly or at least with great self-interest.

It's virtually impossible to always be thinking of other people versus yourself. Your coworkers will fall into this trap for sure. They will talk about themselves. It's true! For this reason, focus on what they need and you'll be seen as a superstar; someone who really listens and understands.

Framing usability problems in the context of another person isn't that hard as I explained previously. The real trick is to connect the dots for the other person. Link it all together for them. Make it a personal story.

This is why you should always be as tangible and hands-on as possible. Keep it concrete. People understand what they can see, hear, taste, touch, and smell. This is why it's best to explain usability in the physical world, from the point of view of the other person. This really is magic. Use their eyes to view the world and paint them a picture; something really easy to grasp.

You've got to always be on the lookout for these opportunities. It's hard to know when an opportunity will manifest but I have faith in you. Listen, you are uniquely positioned to pick the needle out of the haystack. After all, you've got skills and experiences that no one else possesses.

Maximize your potential. Plant the seeds of usability in the minds of those people around you and watch them grow into mighty trees over time. You can do it. Trust me.

Summary of infiltration tips

- Empathy is the number one marketing weapon of UX'ers.
- Pressing the flesh is the best way to interact with others.
- Exploit your ethnographic research skills; target coworkers.
- Appeal to the self-interests of others; learn more about their families, talk about their hopes and dreams along the way.

25

Slush Funds and Funny Money: Be Prepared, Boy Scout

Before you can hit the jackpot,
you have to put a coin in the machine.
~ Flip Wilson

Success is having two things: a little more free time than
you know what to do with and a little more money than
you know what to do with.
~ Courtney Taylor

Summary

This is one of the least well-known secrets of business. There is never enough money when you need it but there are always times where there is extra money to be spent. There are gaps in budgets, cost under runs, plus ups, management reserve funds, and so forth. Often times, this extra money needs to be spent quickly and management often doesn't know how to spend it fast enough. A savvy UX professional will be prepared at all times with three or four project proposals that add value to the bottom line through cost cutting or revenue increases. The engine of the proposals should be tied to UX. It is especially good to have vetted the proposal with others to get their buy in, and to have the team ready to execute.

Jackpot! But Only 5% of the Time

At every single company that I've ever worked for there have been times when money comes pouring in unexpectedly. This has profound implications for your viability as a usability specialist.

You see, most people tend to focus on the negative. They tend to complain that there's not enough money. But in my experience the much bigger problem is not knowing what to do when the river of money flows in. Great business people know exactly what to do when the dam breaks unexpectedly. They are disproportionally rewarded.

I have first-hand experience with this "rainy day" phenomenon. Not only as a recipient of money coming in from executives and project managers, but also as a manager myself dealing with millions of dollars. For example, in the last year alone I have distributed about $250,000 in this manner. Money suddenly became available and it was my job to spend it on something valuable for the business. "Use it or lose it," they said.

Are You Prepared for the Flood?

This situation is a serious challenge for most people. There is a scarcity mentality in most organizations. Plus, most people focus on the negative. They focus when they don't have extra money to spend. We learn to work with less the vast majority of the time so when extra money does flow in, we're not prepared to handle it.

This is all to your advantage. Extra money does fall from the sky from time to time. It's as if you're in a desert wishing for rain. For 360 days out of the year you won't get your wish. But, five days out of the year it does rain. Your wish will come true. Are you prepared when the downpour comes? If you are you'll reap enormous rewards.

In light of all this, I'm going to give you some very strong advice. Create a plan to spend money. I advise you to have 3-5 projects ready to go. Don't just have a wish list, have real business plans ready to go. In short, be ready to strike when the iron is hot. Generate a concrete battle plan so you can scoop that "free" money.

This is an amazing way to grow usability in your organization. It's a story of pennies from Heaven. It's a way to become known as a forward thinking business strategist. It's a catalyst for success.

Fill the Egg Basket with Several Eggs

Now I'm going to give you a special twist on this infiltration tactic. In previous chapters I've discussed working with other people in your organization. I've talked about getting to know people. I've talked about communicating with them face-to-face, and building strong relationships. You're going to capitalize on this investment, and build on the foundation.

As you're building your proposals and you're waiting for your rainy day to arrive, you'll want to spend time doing research in your organization. You're going to look for small but growing projects, but especially ones that could use some usability love. Every company has little projects that are ready to explode. I encourage you to get people talking. Get them to tell you about their projects that need money and attention. Find the ones that would greatly benefit from an injection of user experience. That's your sweet spot.

There's another step to keep in mind. You're going to craft a rough draft of a proposal based on the conversations you're having. You're going to pass these proposals by the people who you've been working with for their approval. And, you're going to get their buy in.

Build a support network. Find champions for your projects so they can take your case forward without your help. They might also be the first to hear of extra money that's available. This is the power of your network. This is why you want that exposure.

Don't just build one proposal; build four or five of them. Have an entire portfolio of potential projects. I suggest working with different areas of your company and different people whenever possible. This increases your opportunities and spreads the risk around. It's very likely the size, scope, and nature of the projects will be different by doing this. This is smart because you never know the true nature of the jackpot until it hits you.

If You Don't Ask, You Don't Know

Very often this extra money is hidden from your view. That means that you need to periodically probe to find out if it's there and available. You absolutely need to know the money people. You need to know how to ask in a subtle way if there are opportunities coming up.

Along a similar vein, it's in your best interest to note the accounting cycles of your organization. At the end of the fiscal year, for example, there might be a lot of pressure to spend or otherwise invest money. I'm telling you to understand your business for the sake of growing your usability empire. Fiscal cycles drive many business decisions.

Never be afraid to tell project managers and executives that you have a portfolio of potential projects. Of course, this means that you need to have your homework done. It means you need to have a strong support network and people to back you up. But, if you've done these things as I've been suggesting, by all means let decision-makers know that you have something in your back pocket ready to go.

Falling Rock Zone

In using these tactics I do have some cautions. If this money does flow into you, it's likely that there are strings attached. For example, you might have a killer deadline looming over you. If we look at the example of money coming in at the end of the fiscal year, you might have a severe time squeeze. But again, this is exactly why you need a portfolio of different projects. Different price points, different customers, different time frames, and so forth. Your portfolio needs to be diverse just like your investment portfolio.

A related caution is that you must execute brilliantly. You won't just be an add-on to a project, you'll actually own and drive the project. There will be a lot of focus and pressure to succeed.

I have faith in you, but you will be on the firing line. This is yet another reason to have a strong network of people to work with in your organization. And not only your own team, but quite literally the people that have helped to build the business cases with you. Even better, find some champions in the outside world; customers. They'll help you get through the flood. But you already knew that, right?

Summary of infiltration tips

- You can pluck money from the money tree when it appears.
- But, you need a portfolio of UX projects in your back pocket.
- Find the money people and get them talking; know their needs.
- When given this "gift money" be sure to execute brilliantly.

26

Making The Case
for Case Studies

The best portraits are perhaps those in which there is a slight mixture of caricature; and we are not certain that the best histories are not those in which a little of the exaggeration of fictitious narrative is judiciously employed. Something is lost in accuracy; but much is gained in effect. The fainter lines are neglected; but the great characteristic features are imprinted on the mind forever.
~ Thomas Babington Macaulay

Not being able to govern events, I govern myself, and apply myself to them, if they will not apply themselves to me.
~ Michel de Montaigne

Summary

The best kind of case study is one that inspires others. It touches the heart. So, if you are interested in getting others interested in user experience you should determine what would resonate with the audience. Focus on the passion of the story first and user experience second. A great case study will also make good business sense. To have the case study sink its hooks into management, especially upper management, try to demonstrate serious bottom line value. Of course, if possible, the value will be directly attributed to usability, interaction design, information architecture, and the like. Avoid trendy case studies. They are fast food for the mind where the value quickly fades. Come back to the case study in your writings and conversations and be sure to highlight the value of UX again and again.

Be The Historian

Every company has its own culture. Every company has its own stories as well. These stories inspire people. And, these stories might be the foundation on which the entire success of the business has been built.

You'll often hear these stories in small to medium businesses, usually something related to what the founder did in the early days. It might be a matter of great customer service. Or, it might be some major challenge that took the organization to the brink of death. The stories are right there in front of you, if you're paying attention.

If you can't find these stories documented anyplace then make it your job to get them written down. I've previously talked about controlling the written word. When you own the documents, you own the history. Further, people will associate you with those stories just because you're the historian. This builds good karma and you'll use that to your advantage as I describe below.

Transform Stories in Case Studies and Testimonials

A case study is really nothing more than a story with facts and details added for good measure. A case study will have a specific context and a deliberate lesson, or takeaway. Perhaps I'm admitting that case studies are nothing more than business stories.

Nevertheless, I encourage you to transform "fluffy" stories into concrete case studies. Make the story one that serves as a lesson to other people. Note that you can adjust the story so that it reflects the perspective of the person or department that you're working with. For example, if you're working with marketing, a success story, which has been transformed into a case study, will revolve around marketing and customers. Of course in all cases you'll include something about usability or the user experience. Therein lies the infiltration tactic.

By the way, you don't have to write the case studies yourself. You can give people a simple framework and let them go hog wild. Give them examples of other stories you've put together. Or, you can do an interview and extract a lot of the information easily and effectively. Just be sure to ask smart questions. Content generation like this is a snap. In fact, it's fun.

You can also use some judo here. Marketing and sales departments are always looking for good news stories to share with other people, especially potential customers. Create your own story or case study and present it to these teams. Demonstrate your value. Make it blatantly obvious that usability and user experience play a big role in the success of your organization. If you need to write this out for them, by all means do it! It's like issuing a high impact press release. It generates serious goodwill.

Make Those Case Studies Hit Home

The best case studies are the ones that are the most personal. They're the ones that have humanity cooked into them. Virtually everyone loves a smiling baby. Everyone loves to hear about lottery winners. And of course, everyone loves it when you mention their name and talk about their family. Keep these things in mind as you are creating your case studies. Inject some personality. Be human.

Don't just bog people down what data and details. Don't just explain the features. Tell people exactly how you're helping the customer. Make it tangible; make it visceral if you can.

In essence, what you're trying to do is create a case study or testimonial that's based on what you've learned by working with other customers. In the hands of a salesperson or marketer, your case study this will be golden.

Tell people that they can use your case studies. Encourage them to edit and adjust as needed. That doesn't mean lying or fabrication, it means shaping the message in a way that provides the maximum value.

If you're handing material to sales and marketing, then let them do their jobs. If you don't inject enough emotion or if you don't pack enough of a punch, trust me, they'll do it for you. If you give them the right material to work with they'll create something amazing.

Traditional Stories Versus Flash-in-the-Pan

I encourage you to go with stories and case studies that have been around your company for quite some time. If something's been around for a while, then it's probably golden. It's also sticky; it's memorable.

Stick with data and metrics that people understand, and that are based on some core truth inside the company. For example, you might find that over the years customers repeatedly tell you the same thing about your products. "We love how your widget is so easy to use, even though you've added more and more features." Wrap those stories – those traditions – within a usability blanket. In short, stay away from fads and stick with what's tried-and-true.

I'm telling you this because I've seen some people create case studies that are basically junk food for the mind. They're only good for a few months or perhaps one trade show. You want to construct something that is high impact and will last over time.

I've ensured that my case studies are successful by testing them with many different people. That's right, I test my documentation. I whip off a quick outline based on the facts and details that I can find. Then, I inject and augment the story with an eye for usability details. Finally, I let others review what I have done.

If I don't get a reaction I go back to the drawing board. I'm looking for a strong positive reaction, not just some brief comments. I'm looking for passion. I'm looking for the fire that makes case studies insanely powerful and compelling.

I'm not talking about fabrication or creating fantasies. I'm talking about creating compelling case studies based on facts but adding a healthy dose of usability along the way. This is such a great way to inject usability into your business. It works like a charm and it doesn't take much work.

Summary of infiltration tips

- Capture stories but then convert them to case studies.
- A case study or testimonial should be concrete and visceral.
- Marketing and sales departments love case studies; exploit this.
- Use case studies that represent the core of the organization, but inject usability where appropriate for serious UX infiltration.

27

Just Keep Asking Questions That Relate to User Experience

*If you are not moving closer to what you want in sales
(or in life), you probably aren't doing enough asking.*
~ Jack Canfield

*A major stimulant to creative thinking is focused questions. There is
something about a well-worded question that often penetrates to the
heart of the matter and triggers new ideas and insights.*
~ Brian Tracy

Summary

Rather than trying to offer solutions and suggestions, get people thinking about UX by asking the right questions. If done right, you can ask questions that you can answer via UX. You can make it clear that there are gaps in projects by digging into certain topics, just be sure that your questions have answers if you take this approach.

Stop, Look, and Listen

Much of what I've explained so far depends on your control of words, language, and documentation. I've discussed how you should be producing and controlling content. Maybe you feel like I've made some big assumptions, like it's your job to provide solutions and answers to everything under the sun. But there's something strange about this. It's as if I think you're a mind reader or that you already have requirements. That's a tall order don't you think?

I'll be the first to say that it's impossible to know everything. There are too many things that are going to be outside your domain of expertise. For example, if you work in a manufacturing company you might have very little knowledge of electrical or mechanical engineering. It's next to impossible to know what to say or to do when interacting with people from these organizations. You can't master all things.

159

I'm going to clear things up. You don't have to be brilliant at all things. You just need to look into your UX toolbox. As it turns out, you are uniquely positioned to gather requirements and to understand what's unspoken in your business. And, you're an expert at understanding what other people want and need. Because you're probably a researcher, or least familiar with research principles, you're going to love this next infiltration tactic. Let's go!

The Power of Active Listening

What you're going to do is quite simple. Just start asking questions. Lots and lots of questions. Like any other research, the more preparation you do, the more you'll achieve. But it's not hard to prepare. You know exactly what you're trying to accomplish. The objective is to get usability into the minds and hearts of the people in your company. You goal is clear and the questions you ask will make this happen, almost through osmosis.

When you ask people questions, you force them to engage you. You force them to really think and connect the dots. It also makes them feel good and important that you actually care about what they. Most people enjoy this kind of attention. It's like giving your coworker an intellectual hug. "I value what you're saying!"

It isn't too hard to ask leading questions. What I mean is that you can ask questions that generate comments about customers. If you really plan ahead and think it through you'll understand that you can ask questions that extract usability stories. That's the raw material for your usability case studies. It all starts by asking smart questions.

Wonderful Side Effects: Finding New Business

Another advantage of asking a lot of questions and pressing the flesh is that you will find genuine needs for user experience consulting. In other words, you can find gaps. You can find projects and teams to work on. You'll see exactly where you can add significant value. Talk to rich people! What I mean is that you should talk to people in departments that have money and influence. I've talked about dog projects and star projects previously. Don't forget my advice, which is that you want to work with the stars. So here I'm telling you to interview the players on the star teams. Move with the upward trend.

Fresh, Hot, Free Survey

Here's another effective tactic I've utilized. I've done this 3-4 times and I just love it. What I do is ask many different people in many different organizations the same set of questions. In essence, I'm conducting a survey. I then use this data to construct various business cases. For example, in one situation, I gathered some very strong data that indicated that a usability lab was needed. This was news to me, but once I got the results parsed, it was so obvious.

I was able to gather financial data, project requirements, customer requests, and more to justify the lab. I actually used the material to write a popular internal whitepaper, which included the recommendation for a usability lab.

Testing, Testing: Can You Hear Me?

As a quick reminder, be sure to be an active listener. Don't ask questions for the sake of asking questions. Instead, ask a question and really give the other person a chance to run with it. Keep them focused and keep your ears open.

Remember, it's your mission is to inject usability into your organization. You're reading this book to learn tactics and this one is especially powerful. Yet its power diminishes if you're not actively and genuinely interested in what the other person is saying. And of course, you must document everything. Write it all down. That provides you with leverage and control when you need it the most.

Summary of infiltration tips

- Don't just produce content, consume it with vigor and passion.
- Just by asking questions you'll establish great relationships.
- Active listening is essential; allow other people to rant and rave.
- Prepare, ask questions, take notes, then write a whitepaper.

28

Dive Into Requirements and Proposals

User experience is everything. It always has been, but it's still undervalued and under-invested in. If you don't know user-centered design, study it. Hire people who know it. Obsess over it. Live and breathe it. Get your whole company on board.
~ Evan Williams

One of the things stupid people do is this: Person A (aka Mr. stupid) writes a requirements document. He makes it super detailed and 50 pages long. He then throws it blindly over a wall (thud!) to person B and says "Do this."
~ Scott Berkun

Summary

Organizations are dynamic and flexible. Get in tune with the changes so that you can inject UX into proposals and requirements documents as the opportunities arise. Similarly, wiggle your way onto proposal teams so you can steer everyone toward UX. Become a requirements guru while also understanding both the language and needs of the business office. When possible, help your organization interpret requirements from a UX point of view. Consider yourself a translator. Generally speaking, do what you can to demonstrate the value of UX at the front end of projects, which is exactly why it is important to be on proposal teams and why you should strive to be involved in the requirements activities in your organization.

Tune In, Follow the Changes, Be Ready

You, your peers and your management are all part of an evolving organism. Power shifts in odd ways in most organizations. Some folks rise quickly while others fall, often for no clear reason. Likewise, interpretation of requirements will shift as human resources shift.

163

To understand how to align UX with the requirements and to the people in your organization, you have to keep your finger on the pulse of those around you. The insight is that requirements and proposals are fluid because the humans interacting with these things are fluid.

Proposals O-Rama

I cannot stress strongly enough that you should try to get on proposal teams. These teams usually work directly with customers. And, the sales organization is heavily involved so they have a very good idea how your organization plans to provide a solution. This is your chance to rub elbows with important folks. It's also your opportunity to get in on the ground floor of a project. That means that you can inject UX ideas all over the place, like a little devil. You can make it clear how UX saves time and money, improves quality, drives up customer satisfaction, and so on.

By being on a proposal team, you can help everyone understand that a solid user experience will drive up the chances for mission success and reduce risk. This is music to the ears of management. Furthermore, in the spirit of being sly, you can encourage the customer to ask for a solid UX. You can egg people on such that they talk a lot about usability, information architecture, and the like.

On a recent project, I was involved in putting together a large proposal. Fortunately, I was invited to join the team early so I had the opportunity to shape the overall thinking and direction of the proposal. Again and again I asked the customer garden path questions about the user experience. For example, I asked about the pain they had been feeling with their help desk. They in turn asked how to prevent or minimize that pain. The answer, of course, was the application of a few usability tricks, including a simple ethnographic study. When I provided these answers, the customer pretty much demanded that we include UX as part of our proposal. Not only did this set our proposal apart from competing proposals but it also injected UX thinking into the proposal itself. Rock on!

By the way, in all of this activity, consider how you might bring in third party resources, such as consultants. Sometimes you can get a high level of UX synergy if you can pull in outside resources at the proposal stage. For a small investment you can get a pretty high return. My advice is to bring UX thinkers to the party, if you have that power.

Become a Requirements Master for Your Organization

If you don't understand how proposals are put together and if you don't understand how to develop a good set of requirements, get cracking now. There is a ton of great information available on this topic. In my opinion, it isn't critical that you follow formal rules and processes or that you fly by the seat of your pants. It all depends on your customers and your organization. However, I will say that bigger projects drive formality whereas smaller ones drive informality. My main advice is to keep asking questions, especially ones about user experience. Dig on those pain points, which are almost always tied to human issues versus technical issues.

Although potentially mind numbing, I suggest that you find some time to bone up on how the business office operates in relation to proposals and requirements. The business office handles proposals, terms and conditions, contract negotiations, and so on. Learn the tools of their trade and take at least a partial interest in their artifacts such as Rough Order of Magnitude (ROM), Basis of Estimate (BOE), Service level Agreement (SLA), Request for Proposal (RFP), and so forth. In smaller organizations this is much less necessary but it's still a good idea to see how everything on the business side operates since it does impact the proposal delivery and the project requirements.

Help Them with Their Maps

Requirements are maps and you are the cartographer. As usual, spend time understanding the requirements and the customer demands. Treat your material like a map, chart the course, and then pass everything along to the designers and developers. Get out of the way. Let them fly the plane. You're a co-pilot but you can adjust the course even though you aren't actually in control.

The truth is that requirements are never good enough. Even when they're great they're not really great. I only think that I've heard one developer ever complain that requirements were too explicit. So, take advantage of this weakness and help your development friends. Dig and dig until you get what they need, and of course, add some UX spice. Even injecting one or two small UX improvements will add value and edge UX into your organization.

Thinking this through, you'll probably realize that you're also a translator. It's true! You're the first level interpreter because you're one or two steps away from the customer, and you're interacting with the folks creating the requirements. In turn, designers and developer's interpret what you give them. This is an insight: you actually have two opportunities to inject UX into a project by working smartly with designers and developers. It's a smashingly good opportunity.

Demonstrate UX Value at the Front End of Projects

If you've been in the UX game for any time, you know that UX is often only considered near the end of the project. UX is seen as magic fairy dust to be sprinkled on a project to improve the chances of its success. This is pretty frustrating.

Take a stand. Don't let others dictate when and how UX makes sense. That is your job and your obligation. Demonstrate that you have what it takes to filter out bad ideas early. Illustrate the benefits of UX early in the process through better requirements gathering and analysis.

Along these lines, consider taking leadership positions whenever possible so that you have more leverage. If you think you are a small potato in your organization then that is exactly what you'll be. Go large, shoot for the stars. Leaders are included earlier than those who are not. That means more influence and greater chances of getting UX cooked into proposals and requirements.

Summary of infiltration tips

- As organizations change, watch for opportunities to inject UX, particularly with project proposals and requirements documents.
- Get onto proposal teams, especially if you can take leadership positions because this will give you the power to add UX.
- Consider yourself a requirements translator; discuss the user experience point of view when it makes sense.

29

You Have Mad Skillz, Apply Them

A lot of people in our industry haven't had very diverse experiences. They don't have enough dots to connect, and they end up with very linear solutions, without a broad perspective on the problem. The broader one's understanding of the human experience, the better designs we will have.
~ Steve Jobs

No matter what age you are, or what your circumstances might be, you are special, and you still have something unique to offer. Your life, because of who you are, has meaning.
~ Barbara De Angelis

Summary

You know how to think about end users and customers. You know how to gather data and get answers to tough questions. Why not apply these skills to your work environment, including management and your peers? Find out what makes these people tick. Find ways to help them. Find ways to make them successful. As you are doing this, continually work with people to understand the value of UX. You don't need to explain the processes, tools, or techniques; instead you need to focus on value. Start with your resume to find success. There are hidden gems in there we're going to expose.

The Skills You Have

If you haven't updated your resume recently I suggest that you do so right now. No, not because your job is threatened or your career is in jeopardy. Quite the opposite, actually.

I'd like you to think about the skills that you have as a usability professional. The range of skills and aptitudes for the average usability professional is usually quite large. In just a moment I'm going to explain the significance of this. For now, just realize that you're not like everyone else. You've got an incredible bag of tricks that I'm going to help you use to grow your empire.

Your Resume is a Gold Mine

Consider for a moment why you even have a resume. And, think for a moment about what happens when you update your resume. In essence, what you're doing is a full skills assessment. You can leverage this resume review process in such a way that you'll learn a new user experience infiltration tactic.

As you're reviewing and updating your resume, I want you to think about one thing: the value you bring to an organization. If you're not thinking about the bottom line in relation to your usability skills, you're selling yourself short. You offer a lot more than your technical skills.

Here's an analogy. A Java programmer might only explain his programming skills on his resume, with very little else provided. He might describe his team, organizations that he's worked for, and the types of applications that he's built too. But, he doesn't explain that his latest project, driven by his outstanding skills, resulted in cost savings of $2.3 million. The programmer is selling himself short because he's not connecting his work to the bottom line.

In that example above I hope you see what's really going on. I want you to avoid that trap, where you only describe what you do and how you do it, not your bottom-line impact. I'm trying to show you that as a usability professional you're much more than just a person with some skills and a toolbox. Further, the resume exercise that I described is meant to make you reflect on the true value you provide. In short, map your skills to the bottom line.

You're a Snowflake

I've spent time talking about your resume to get you thinking not only about your skills and your value to the organization, but also to get you to realize that you are unique. With these unique skills and talents, you're going to help people in your business in ways that you haven't even considered. I'm talking about helping your peers, managers, executives, project leaders, and other folks who will work with you. They will help you inject user experience in the organization.

In a previous chapter I talked about the importance of asking a lot of smart questions questions. I talked about gathering requirements by just talking and then actively listening. Lots of listening.

But, you have other skills. This is why I wanted you to spend some time reviewing your resume and thinking about the full range of skills you possess. For example, you know how to conduct research. Therefore, you can help people in your organization conduct studies. You can analyze data and provide recommendations. You're able to get your head around complex problems and you're probably pretty good at explaining those complex problems in ways that make sense to everyone. You might even have unique solutions for those problems that non-usability professionals simply would not have.

These are high value, significant skills. They are "natural" to you but not to many other people in your company. Here's the punchline: Don't sell usability, sell your high impact skills. UX'ers are smart. You're smart. Exploit your talents.

The Foot in the Door Tactic, Revealed

You've got empathy, great listening skills, and the ability to wrap your head around some of the toughest issues in your organization. When you talk to other people you don't have to sell them on usability or user experience. Simply sell them on these abilities. Consider this a way to get your foot in the door. You never have to say anything about usability or user experience. As I've explained before, there's no need for UX jargon.

Here's the business truth. If you can provide solutions to difficult problems, and if you can have a true bottom-line impact, then you'll be in great demand. It doesn't matter that you're a usability specialist. Let them call you whatever they want. Provide value, get your foot in the door, then slowly inject UX into the organization. Boil that frog!

Hopefully now you see why I ran you through the resume exercise early in this chapter. The exercise of reviewing and updating your resume can produce nuggets of inspiration.

Now you have the framework to understand what your skills are in relation to the needs of the business. You've done that mapping, right? Remember, it's not just that you can conduct pluralistic walk-throughs, heuristic analyses, usability testing, and more. Instead, it's that you're helping real people solve real problems. Your value isn't your label. It isn't your methods or tools alone. It's your brainpower applied in the right way, to the right problems, at the right time.

Go get 'em, tiger!

Summary of infiltration tips

- You have unique skills: research, analysis, strategy, empathy.
- Review and update your resume; think about the bottom-line.
- Once in the door and they're "sold" on you, start injecting UX.

30

Why Take the Test When You Can Take the Train?

I cannot teach anybody anything, I can only make them think.
~ Socrates

The greatest challenge to any thinker is stating the problem in a way that will allow a solution.
~ Bertrand Russell

Summary

Many people seem to think that user experience is all about doing research and performing tests. Many think it's all about data analysis. Sometimes the best way to cook UX into a company is via training. If you have the skills and opportunity, run a brown bag lunch and provide people with tools and techniques they can use on their own (i.e., coffee cup or hallway usability is great example of this). Or, if that won't work, find ways to get developers and designers into training classes provided by top notch UX folks.

Get Talking

I've talked to a lot of usability professionals over the years. One thing that amazes me is that folks have not done much training in their organizations. In light of this, I'm going to explain how to use a simple training technique to get UX into your company. It's so easy!

Because you do usability work, I know that you've probably got great interpersonal skills. Very likely you also have strong presentation skills. You need to capitalize on the strength.

It goes without saying that if you have a fear of public speaking or you don't have strong presentation skills, then you must start working on this immediately. Your ability to effectively to communicate in public is a key determinant of your success as a usability professional. Although you can make progress one-to-one with people, to really pack a punch you need to hit an entire audience. You need to interact with groups of people. You need to hear them speak with one another. A key reason for this is to understand the true issues in your organization. You won't get this one-on-one. It needs to be in a larger group where people feel free to share their thoughts, issues, and concerns.

From this point forward I'm going to assume that you either have strong public speaking skills or that you've made a note to dedicate yourself to improving this critical skill.

Active interaction is what gives you the most leverage to influence and persuade others. Also keep in mind that virtually all user experience infiltration tactics depend on some form of interaction. Putting it yet another way, if you're not a strong writer then you must be a strong speaker. It's essential.

The Power of the Brown Bag Lunch

Most people in an organization will probably think that usability specialists just do research and perform tests. We're seen as being academics in the corporate world. Of course this isn't always true but it's what I've seen time and again. If you're not seen as an academic, consider yourself very lucky.

At this point I want to expose the next user experience infiltration tactic to you. What you're going to do is run a brown bag lunch session. If you're not familiar with the brown bag lunch idea, here it is. You set aside half an hour to an hour and ask people to bring their own lunches. You pick some hot topic that everyone cares about and then you just talk about it. You can take a facilitator role, or you can provide concrete solutions, roadmaps, generic problem-solving techniques, and the like.

This is real magic. It's also a huge opportunity for you. Brown bag lunches are usually very informal. People talk a lot; they interrupt, they get emotional. Because of this, you're able to gather requirements about what the organization needs in relation to usability and user experience. So much is exposed about the personalities, the challenges, the politics and more.

Everyone wins. Not only do you get a chance to see how people interact you get to learn about their issues. You also get a chance to influence them. That's what this book is all about, right? Since you set the brown bag lunch up, you control the agenda. You're able to talk about whatever you want. Of course I very strongly recommend that you avoid jargon and that you focus on the wants and needs of your audience. Be genuine. Be legitimately helpful.

The Brown Bag Tutorial

One of the best tactics for running a great brownbag is to do a simple tutorial. Combine this tutorial with a quick interactive exercise and you'll have a winner on your hands.

Here's a note of caution. Just because brown bags are casual and informal, I'm not giving you an excuse for lack of preparation. In fact, treat brown bags very seriously, as if you're interacting with real customers or perhaps your executive team. It's this dedication and focus that will make your brownbag session an overwhelming success.

Hint: If you can gather up problems and concerns before the brownbag, you'll be a champ. For example, if Jake the Programmer is having problems with labels in his web application perhaps you can provide a tutorial on developing effective groupings and labels. Help the team; give them a simple step-by-step battle plan. The point is that you want to ground your tutorial in something practical if you want maximum impact. Jake will deeply appreciate your help. The team will appreciate the brownbag. This builds up goodwill that you can leverage at a later time. All around, this is a winning tactic.

Coffee Cup Usability Training

Along a similar vein I recommend what I call coffee cup usability training. Before I explain this, let me remind you about something I covered in an earlier chapter. Specifically, I talked about the development of an elevator speech. Keep that in the back of your mind as I explain this.

What you're going to do is use your elevator pitch in the context of a casual hallway conversation. You might do this at the water cooler or as you're grabbing some coffee. What you'll do is give a 30 second to one-minute tutorial on usability in relation to an issue that someone is explaining to you. Honestly, this can be as simple as giving some simple advice to someone on a project: "Hey, why not try watching someone use that web application you developed. What I do is give them a simple task and then I just watch them work. I don't say much, I just take notes as they give it a whirl!"

Of course you have to exercise good judgment. You don't want to water down UX too much since it'll do more harm than good. But it gets your foot in the door. It's also very practical and will lead to other conversations. If nothing else, you've planted a seed in the mind of the other person. If they really get stuck and they need help, they might just seek you out for help. That's exactly what you're trying to do. You're trying to provide bottom line value, and you're positioning yourself as an expert.

If you have a coffee cup usability conversation then you also want to follow up with an email or another face-to-face conversation. Demonstrate to the other person you have genuine concern for their challenges. You can insert a very subtle message about usability or user experience when you do this. Focus on the solution that the usability method or methods you've employed. Again, keep it casual and focus on the problem first, usability second. That's the key here.

Summary of infiltration tips

- If you're not a good writer, then you need to be a good speaker.
- Training is an excellent way to get people to learn about UX.
- Set up a brownbag luncheon and help people; feed their minds.
- Use a coffee cup usability training to get your foot in their door.

31

Corporate PsyOps, Perception Management and Propaganda

*Miracles seem to rest, not so much upon faces or voices or
healing power coming suddenly near to us from far off,
but upon our perceptions being made finer so that for a
moment our eyes can see and our ears can hear that which
is about us always.*
~ Willa Cather

*The goal of modern propaganda is no longer to transform
opinion but to arouse an active and mythical belief.*
~ Jacques Ellul

Summary

This technique is all about taking the time to manage the perceptions of UX. It is generally less important to explain what it is than what it offers. It is imperative to declare UX success when you see it. You cannot assume that other people understand the value of user-centered design. You have to make it explicit and overt but be careful about overplaying it. Consider that you are always on display as the UX guru, as the leader of a great movement. If you want to be taken seriously, don't go to work wearing flip flops and baggy shorts. I'm not trying to tell you how to live your life, but consider how others think about what you say based on how you look. Perceptions matter. You know it.

Bury User Experience in Your Words

I've often stated that perception is more important than reality. This is especially true in business. While you do need a high quality product or service, it's even more important to make sure that people are seeing things appropriately. They need to feel and understand the value.

I'm bringing this up because usability is misunderstood, more often than not. Usability has a perception problem and I want to help you rectify the situation. In previous chapters I've talked about the importance of documentation and communication. You'll use your writing and speaking skills to ensure that you're fairly represented.

My point is that in addition to controlling the language, you're controlling how people think about UX. Words have deep meanings and you can sneak UX into your company in subtle ways. Use a lot of words that are associated with UX, but not UX specific. For example, you might label something as being "customer friendly" in a report. You can then define "customer friendly" in a way that pushes your UX agenda. This isn't to be devious; it's just plain practical. You're simply using words and phrases related to UX. You're adjusting perceptions by using language effectively. It's a great tactic.

Sidebar: For some reason usability professionals have a justification mentality. They feel they must justify their existence. They feel they must beg, acquiesce, and defer to others. Many people I've talked to feel very stressed and threatened. They feel marginalized in their organizations. The more pressure they feel, the more they tend to fall back on explaining what they do versus why it's so important to the organization. Again, this is absolutely a perception problem.

It's What You Offer That Matters

Usability offers very direct, tangible outputs. It's the presentation of these inputs that matter. This is the difference you can make in the organization, and the value that usability ultimately offers. Talk about those benefits whenever you can.

I'm saying that there's usually very little point in explaining how you get your work done. Card sorting, heuristic analyses, remote usability testing – how these things are done just doesn't mean much to most people. Yet, the results you provide mean everything. The outputs that you generate are the diamonds.

So when I say you need to manage expectations I'm saying that you need to spend more time discussing these outputs and their impact on the organization, not how you got them.

What You Need to Read Next

This might sound odd, but I recommend that you do some reading on propaganda. Similarly, learn about public relations tactics and methods that I've touched on in this book. You can use these for your own sake to manage expectations of those around you.

I'm also going to recommend that you learn more about psychological operations by the military. You might laugh at this but I've learned a lot from this research. The government has poured millions of dollars into "psych ops" and I'm telling you that it's your duty to exploit what they've done. And no, I'm not talking about dirty tactics. I'm talking about basic principles of how to get groups of people to better understand you and appreciate the value that you bring to the table.

You Are What You Wear

If you want to be taken seriously and as a professional, then you're going to have to consider your appearance and mannerisms. I'm not talking about being shallow or materialistic, but I am talking about putting your best foot forward. People do judge you based on what you wear, what you say, and how you act. Play the part of a genuine UX professional. You are an emissary of user experience in your organization. As such, you're always on display.

I'm guessing that some people will have a negative reaction to some of the things I've stated in this chapter. That's perfectly reasonable and I understand where you're coming from. At the same time, I do ask you to have an open mind about the infiltration tactics I provided above. I'm not telling you how to think and I'm not telling you what to wear to work, but I am giving you real world advice on perception management.

Some people would say I'm giving you lessons in expectation management as well. These skills are valuable no matter what you do in the future and no matter what organization you're working in.

Summary of infiltration tips

- You can adjust how people think about the valuable work you do.
- Discuss your bottom line value if you want to attract attention.
- Read up on propaganda, psych ops, and public relations.
- Dress, speak and act like a professional to gain respect.

32

Networking Nuances: Working the Herd

We herd sheep, we drive cattle, we lead people. Lead me, follow me, or get out of my way.
~ General George S. Patton

People are like dirt. They can either nourish you and help you grow as a person or they can stunt your growth and make you wilt and die.
~ Plato

Summary

Find like-minded folks and build a coalition. Grow your support system. Seek out folks with sincere empathy for users and customers. Be sure to talk with folks that really don't care about UX so you understand the state of the business. They'll also keep you in touch with issues related to timelines, costs, development problems, potential bugs, and so forth. But your real focus needs to be on people that are friendly to the value of usability and user experience.

Let 1,000 Flowers Bloom, Then Let Me Pick My Favorites

We live in an age of diversity. We've been trained to believe that we must include everyone in everything we do, as if it's their natural right. We're told to respect others and to adjust our lives to accommodate them. But is this always fair? Is it always good for you personally and professionally? Is it always good for your business? My answer is simple: I don't think it is.

Before you throw up your arms...

I do value what other people think. I look for opinions and ask for constructive criticism. This is part of my effort to be an effective usability specialist and consultant. I strive to be the best in what I do. For this very reason it's not realistic, nor is it productive, to reach out to everyone. Furthermore, I'm very selective when it comes to the people I work with and the opinions they offer. The people around you are responsible for 90% of your success, especially if you're a leader.

The Nodes in the Network

I'm a strong advocate for working with a small group of people that are oriented towards success. I'm always looking for the best team possible. If there is no strong team, I want to help create it. That's my kind of challenge. I want to work with the smartest people possible. That's why I actively seek out people who seem to have an affinity for customer service, empathy, and a passion for growing the business. I also seek out mentors. I know that I have blindspots and weaknesses. Many! That's precisely why I seek out people who have deep knowledge. I also want them to share my passion – directly or indirectly – for usability and user experience.

I'm biased towards people in sales, service, marketing, product development, and engineering. I'm also fond administrative assistants because they're a direct pipeline to customers as well as executives. The one thing that should stand out to you about this list of people is that they directly interface with customers. That's key in my mind.

On a personal level, I'm friendly with people in finance, operations, legal, and the like. But I'm going to be honest with you, these folks are far removed from the customer. They care much less about usability and user experience than the folks I mentioned above. Or, to put it another way, they're internally focused on the organization. I resonate with people on the firing line, the people who directly interact with users.

In summary, I'll talk to anyone in the organization. I maintain a good feel for timelines, new projects, development problems, and the like. I keep my ear the floor for anything that might be valuable to the organization, but of course I have a bias towards things related to usability.

Connecting Some of the Dots

In a previous chapter I discussed the topic of creating a portfolio of potential user experience projects. You'll want to pass this portfolio by your mentors as well as other individuals that you respect. You're not looking for head nods in agreement; you're looking to get genuine feedback. Don't be afraid to put your projects to the test with your trusted peers and advisers. That's why they're there.

As you're building this network of trusted friends and colleagues in the organization consider the following. Treat this as a serious business activity for the sake of boosting usability in your organization. In the previous chapter I discussed coffee cup usability training and brownbag lunches. I'm telling you to take it one step further but with some formality. Document what you're doing and you can take it to your leadership at the right time. Get credit for being a mentor as well as a student. This shows your personal and professional dedication but also paves the way for management to see you as a forward thinker and usability leader. This certainly can't hurt you during performance appraisals either

Create Management Support for Usability

This is a radical maneuver but it can deliver incredible rewards. If you're having difficulty working with management, and especially your first line manager, you might need to put together a business case for moving to another department. Create support by changing your situation. Take control of your career by changing context.

The reason for a radical change is that a strong manager, along with management support, is a major catalyst for growth. No management support, no growth. Position yourself in the organization and you'll reap the rewards.

Don't let the organization command your future. Take hold of your career. For example, it might be worth your time to take a horizontal transfer into the marketing department. You'll meet new people and you'll learn new ways to operate in your organization that you never dreamed of. Plus as you learned earlier, it doesn't matter what you call user experience, what matters are the results. No one says you can't transport your methods and techniques. In fact, UX skills are highly flexible and portable. That's a million dollar fact.

How Can You Break Through Senior Management Roadblocks?

Here's the short answer: Become a senior manager. Seek to become an executive. You can do it by moving away from your current UX position. You might be shocked by my words. I know this sounds like heresy but listen, I don't know any CEOs who started off in usability. Do you?

For the record, many senior executives start off in sales and marketing. So listen up, if you make a radical jump you might be on the path to the corner office. I'll admit that saying I'm saying this tongue-in-cheek but just imagine what you could do with those budgets and staff.

Two Special Skills: Knowing Who You Are and What You Want

This is a good place to talk about something I think is really important, especially for early-career usability specialists. Please spend some time thinking about my comments below.

I love usability but I want you to recognize that it could force you into a cul-de-sac. It's also easy to fall prey to a career plateau in UX. The top position you can hold is usability lab manager. Or, if you're organization is big enough, maybe you can move into some sort of director position. There are Chief Experience Officers in some monster companies but they are rare. My point is that your UX career might eventually feel like a dead end.

Does this rattle your cage? Does it get you thinking about big company corporate cultures? Does it make you question what you're doing? Are you feeling frustrated by your lack of professional mobility? If yes, I'm glad for it! It's important to be challenged. You've got to find ways to see the business world with open eyes. You cannot maximize your potential without knowing exactly what you want. Know thyself, usability specialist. If you don't, you'll lose the passion and the flame for helping customers and changing the world.

I'll wrap this up by letting you know that there are many ways that you can align your objectives with the objectives of the company. Don't fret – it's possible to inject user experience principles into an organization from any position that you hold. That's one of the most important pieces to the UX infiltration puzzle. Keep your eyes open.

Summary of infiltration tips

- Don't try to include everyone in your quest for UX domination.
- Surprise! You've got friends in sales and marketing, trust me.
- Consider getting out of the UX field to have the greatest impact.
- If you don't know what you want as a UX'er get cracking on it.

33

Develop Mindshare: If You Can't Do It, Write About It

I would hurl words into this darkness and wait for an echo, and if an echo sounded, no matter how faintly, I would send other words to tell, to march, to fight, to create a sense of hunger for life that gnaws in us all.
~ Richard Wright

To exercise power costs effort and demands courage. That is why so many fail to assert rights to which they are perfectly entitled – because a right is a kind of power but they are too lazy or too cowardly to exercise it. The virtues which cloak these faults are called patience and forbearance.
~ Friedrich Nietzsche

Summary

Surprisingly few UX professionals have considered generating material for their peers in an effort to win them over. If your hands are tied and it is impossible to do usability testing or UX work, find others ways to get the message across. Write about UX. Generate a newsletter, share articles, provide FAQs on the intranet, ask to help with Help documentation, and so on. Get others to seek you out for your writing talents and become a magnet. Help others with their writing and work UX into the mix. The keyboard is the mighty weapon of UX.

Maximize The Inevitable Down Time

In previous chapters I've spent time talking about content generation, document control, use of language, and the like. I'm going to expand on those topics in this chapter. I'm going to give you even more specific infiltration tools.

Before I begin I need to spend a little time giving you proper context. In the corporate world there is a truth. Business is never constant. There ups and there are downs, projects come and go, and the road can be quite rocky. I strongly suggest that you maximize your down time. Those "slow times" are opportunities to invest in UX infiltration.

Review your resume and build your portfolio of user experience projects, but also invest in the tactics that I'm going to explain shortly.

The Newsletter Publishing Tactic

The general idea is that you're going to generate content that will be passively consumed. Here's the first example. You're going to generate a newsletter. If you've taken my advice and you've spent time with people around the organization, you've been able build strong relationships, you're uniquely positioned to create content that will have general appeal. And, you should have been able to get your colleagues excited about your newsletter. They'll read it, forward it, and even provide you with word-of-mouth marketing.

A newsletter does not need to be printed. It can certainly be electronic. It doesn't need to be a long. It can just be an email with a few paragraphs with an important punchline at the end. You can generate this newsletter once per week, once per month or even once per quarter. What matters is that people see you as a communicator and an aggregator of ideas. You'll be seen as a knowledge hub.

As you're generating the newsletter you're going to bake in usability and user experience. I recommend against using jargon for reasons I've discussed previously. There's no point in attempting a frontal assault on your organization with your newsletter. Steady and even will win the race.

Hand Out Useful Articles Like Candy on Halloween

A related tactic is to share articles. This is ripped right out of the pages of the best marketing books in the world. It's tried and true. Again, the effectiveness of this tactic depends on your knowledge of the needs of other people in the organization.

What you're going to do is quite simple. As you find articles online and off-line, you're going to view them through the eyes of other people in your organization. What would they appreciate? What would they like to learn about? What will help them solve a problem? If you find an article or book that helps him in some way, you'll simply pass it along.

Not only are these gestures friendly they also provide you with an opportunity to sneak in a usability message. Perhaps the message is extremely simple and completely unspoken. For example, you might find something on a usability blog like WebWord.com which perfectly explains a solution to a problem that your coworker is facing. Just the fact that the material comes from a usability blog makes this an infiltration tactic. It's subtle but these efforts compound like interest in the bank. Subtle cues and messages will eventually change the thinking as well as the actions of your colleagues.

FAQs and Help Documentation

Here's another thing you can do. I recommend that you volunteer to either generate or update FAQs on your intranet. Similarly, volunteer to help people with their help documentation. Most people do not like to document so this is low hanging fruit for you.

Like the other tactics in this chapter, what you'll do is simply include usability and user experience material in the FAQs and help documentation. This is simple and subtle. You can do this with links, references, sidebars, and so on. You don't need to beat people over the head with usability material. You just need to get it in front of them again and again, from multiple angles.

Production Versus Consumption

If you sat in bed reading books all day you would have a hard time generating wealth. If you went swimming and hiking every day you would get healthy, but your bank account would not grow. You would not have any money to buy food and you'd lose your home. In the same way, if you're only getting smarter about usability over time and you're not contributing to your company, you're not going to grow. This is especially true with respect to the UX infiltration tactics that I've been explaining to you.

You must take action to be helpful. You must offer your services. You need to be constructive; you need to be an architect and a builder. In short, you need to be a juggernaut. You must be an unstoppable forward moving force for the sake of usability. This passion is your fuel. It's what drives all UX infiltration tactics.

Beware! This entails some risk. You're putting yourself on the line and you might get shot down from time to time. You need to make the first move, offer the first handshake, make eye contact, and become engaged with your coworkers just like you do with users in a usability test. You must have a thick skin. Get your ego out of the way, plug your nose, and jump into the deep end. This book will keep you floating. Have confidence. No worries!

Summary of infiltration tips

- All jobs have "lazy time" that you should usefully exploit.
- Write a general appeal newsletter; leverage your network.
- Hand out good articles and books that you find; write articles too.
- Lack of action will kill your infiltration efforts, so keep on pushing.

34

**Lessons Learned Sessions:
Sneak in the User Experience**

The greatest pleasure I know is to do a good action by stealth and have it found out by accident.
~ Charles Lamb

In every adversity there lies the seed of an equivalent advantage. In every defeat is a lesson showing you how to win the victory next time.
~ Robert Collier

Summary

At the conclusion of projects you need to find ways to review what worked and what did not for other people. Invariably, there will be several issues tied to usability, findability, and the like. Use the opportunity to drive a usability spike into the business and get others to consider UX in the future. Be the person that other people look to for improving project management but also UX advice in these sessions.

You Can Have an Impact When the Game is Over

The core of this user experience infiltration tactic is quite simple. You're going to be looking for projects that are coming to a conclusion or at least coming to a halting point. Then you're going to sneak in some UX. You'll enjoy this tactic if you're always getting pulled into projects late in the cycle. "We can add in some usability at the end the project" – yeah right!

It's not possible to always get into a project right at the start. This is especially true if you've just come into a company or you're establishing yourself in the organization. Similarly, you might be a consultant called in to provide support. You might be considered an after thought, which is exactly the reason you're reading this book, right? You want to get traction early in a project whenever possible.

It's been my experience that people either feel really good or really bad about projects. There's a lot of happiness or a ton of negativity. While it's true that people sometimes just muddle through, most times there is a strong emotional attachment. It's this emotional attachment that you're going to capitalize on. We'll dig into this in a moment.

For what it's worth, I've used this approach with success for years. You can be as subtle or as explicit as you would like with this tactic. Use your judgment about how aggressive you need to be. I tend to take it slow and easy, but there have been times where I've really been as busy as a bunny. I've also stuck my neck out more than once but that's what it takes sometimes.

How It Works

What you're going to do is offer to put together a lessons learned session, which is simply a post hoc analysis of the project as a whole. You'll work with the team to understand what worked and what didn't work. If the project was a success then you will focus more on the positive aspects than the negative. You'll be looking for things that you can share with the rest of the organization. You're on an expedition looking for new ideas and concepts; big game hunting.

Conversely, if the project was a failure, you have to figure out why it was so difficult to surmount the challenges. Then you'll provide feedback and recommendations to the team. You may or may not push this information to the rest of the organization.

I am biased. You know from earlier chapters that I like stars more than dogs. To be more precise, I tend to seek out successful projects versus the ones that have flamed out. It's easier to be an evangelist for projects that make customers happy and pull in cash for the business than ones that have exploded. My objective is to inject usability and user experience where it makes sense. Great projects make my life easier, that's the plain truth.

They Will Invite You Next Time

There's another reason why it's so important to put together lessons learned sessions. You'll be seen as a strategist, confidant, and effective cheerleader. They will call you a forward thinker and a person of action. What you're really doing is establishing yourself as a key player on the next project.

By working on a completed project – even one that is 100% done – you're building a bridge to the next project. So what if you're called in late? It's better than not being called in whatsoever. Further, you're turning the "lateness lemon" into lemonade. This tactic is about creating opportunities. You're filling your future work pipeline, just like a good salesman would do.

There's another interesting aspect of this tactic that I'd like you to consider. Many people think projects simply end, when in fact they are rarely ever complete. If you're savvy about business and you have an eye on customers, you'll know the truth in my words. Projects are organic and they always evolve. They grow and grow. If you're a smart farmer, you'll have UX crops in no time.

Here are some specific ideas. You can suggest new product features. You can help to develop a product or service upgrade. You can help the marketing team create an upsell (i.e., higher priced, premium product that compliments the first purchase). You can do these things because you have superior knowledge of customers. Your expertise in user experience has tangible business benefits that you can leverage here for substantial gain, and UX infiltration.

Post Launch Support

Assuming the project is in the market and there's nothing more you can do because it's been launched, there's one more infiltration tactic up my sleeve. Many products cause headaches for customer service and helpdesk teams. Documentation teams also feel pain;

no one likes to write user manuals. Volunteer to assist. Proofreading and editing will be appreciated.

You have the skills and the in-depth knowledge of customers to know exactly what to deliver to improve the overall customer experience. You can help coworkers and customers simultaneously.

Remember that customers provide some of the best requirements after a product or service is launched. By working closely with the customer service department you'll have a direct connection to customers. That provides you with many unique opportunities, such as requirements development, building relationships with potential UX testing participants, and fostering a reputation for customer service. This is all excellent ammunition for your usability efforts.

Summary of infiltration tips

- Seek out projects that are ending, generate lessons learned.
- Use lessons learned sessions to create a bridge to new projects.
- Help marketing and sales; provide intelligence on upselling.

35

Tending the Farm: Mentoring, Internships, Hiring Committees

*I would suggest finding any way possible to watch, learn,
and be involved; make the effort to develop mentoring
relationships whenever possible.*
~ Randy West

*I am convinced that nothing we do is more important than
hiring and developing people. At the end of the day you bet
on people, not on strategies.*
~ Larry Bossidy

Summary

Get involved with any activity that results in getting people into the organization. Be an interviewer. Drive people into the organization by supplying resumes to hiring managers. Once they're in, assist new employees in their careers while showing them the value of UX along the way. Interns are an excellent source of new thinking and they'll be receptive to usability. Note that many interns are willing to work for free in exchange for experience. The bottom line is that if you can bring in fresh blood you can increase the UX in the company.

Three Prong Attack

In this chapter I'm going to describe three tactics that are all related. The central idea is that you're going to position yourself in your organization so that you can influence various human resource decisions. Specifically, I'm talking about helping the organization to bring people in who are keen on usability and user experience. I'm also talking about working with people who have just joined your company. You'll lend your helping hands but also your influence and persuasion. In previous chapters I've discussed playing the role of a mentor.

What I want you to realize is that everyone needs help and support at some point in their career. In fact, most people need help each and every day. It's your job to position yourself in front of these problems, and to take some bullets when you can for the sake of others.

Obviously this builds goodwill and karma, and it builds you a strong reputation, but it also gives you perspective on exactly what these people are facing. Not only can you mentor your coworkers but also you can adjust the mindset that these people have about usability specialists and the value they provide. It's an opportunity to shape their thinking about UX.

Let's say you take up the role of a mentor. You can help your coworker create short and long-term goals. You can help them map out their work and their impact on the bottom line.

Now, here's the infiltration tactic: What you'll do is make one of the goals to learn more about usability and user experience. Certainly you don't have to call it that – you can completely avoid the jargon. You can guide the person in a way that makes them understand and value usability. By the way, you might even find that this person develops a desire to become a usability professional. Stay sharp on that point.

Interns Can Boost Your UX Presence Tremendously

In addition to mentoring, I strongly encourage you to hire interns. They don't even need to work in your department or alongside you. You simply need to influence others to bring them in. In turn, they'll have a favorable disposition towards usability, ergonomics, information architecture, customer satisfaction, and the like. Once again I'm telling you to get in front of the train. My strong recommendation is for you to control the flow of people, and their fresh ideas and perspectives.

If you don't have an internship program why not create one? If you're near a local community college or university, this is a no-brainer. If your company can offer compensation to interns and co-ops all the better, but it isn't necessary. Many students are simply looking for experience and exposure. They're looking to interact with smart people and challenge their assumptions about the workplace. They're also looking to get their foot in the door. Consider the leverage you have just sifting, sorting and reviewing those resumes.

New Life Through Hiring Committees

As companies grow they must hire. With the aging workforce and the attrition, there's a burning need to bring in fresh blood. It will only increase in the next 10-20 years. Organizations also face churn. Keep in mind that even new hires will leave a company; the younger generation is especially keen on employment mobility. The bottom line is that human resource departments face an uphill battle to bring in high quality talent. It isn't going to let up.

For this reason I strongly encourage you to get on hiring committees. If you happen to be a manager or a project leader with some influence, bringing in people with an eye towards usability is in your best interest. It's infiltration at its best.

Control New Employee Documentation

There's something else you can do to augment the tactics above. Many companies have very weak new employee orientation programs. Most new employees feel lost and confused. Many managers are rushed and cannot dedicate time to these new hires, despite the fact that they need them to desperately jump into projects and add value immediately.

What you'll do is help managers with new employee orientation. Many medium and large companies have formal "buddy" programs. Jump on that opportunity. You can help everyone and you can inject usability ideas when you have a lot of influence; when employees are sponges.

I also recommend that you volunteer to make updates to the new employee orientation manual, if there is one. When you make those edits simply add a link to your UX intranet page. Drive traffic to the web pages that you control.

Participant Pool and Riding Those Coattails

There's another reason for being a mentor, working with interns, and helping new employees. These folks are perfect for being participants in your usability tests. In other words, by working with them you establish a pool of people to work with doing UX research.

There is the possibility that they will be biased too much towards usability, but that's a small price to pay. The more important aspect is that by building these relationships you're creating a subject pool that you can easily tap. Bingo!

You're also building a group of UX evangelists. These coworkers will advance in their careers and perhaps pull you along for the ride. You're biasing them so that they'll flow money into your lab and into your team. They might also invite you to be a guest speaker for one of their brownbag luncheons. In short, by helping them they'll create opportunities for you in the months and years ahead.

Earlier I mentioned churn and how the younger generation is devoted to employment mobility. Keeping an eye on your own career is smart, and these new employees might just be able to help you in a pinch. If they happen to leave your organization, you might be able to tag along to find greener pastures. Or they might become either a customer or supplier of your organization, and you'll have a stronger network.

This might ultimately be the way that you break free from your organization if you're frustrated. They might help you spread your wings and become a user experience consultant if you're locked in a huge Fortune 500 company but you want to flee.

Summary of infiltration tips

- Get involved in human resources actions and decisions.
- Become a mentor and help new employees learn the value of UX.
- Help decide which interns get hired; once in, provide assistance.
- Control or otherwise influence new employee orientation material.
- Your future is tied to the people being brought into the company.

36

Slap! Ask Yourself, Is There Better ROI with Something Else?

I wasn't satisfied just to earn a good living.
I was looking to make a statement.
~ Donald Trump

Design is so critical it should be on the agenda of every
meeting in every single department.
~ Tom Peters

Summary

You need to constantly think about the value you can provide to the organization. You need to compare that value to the value of other activities, methods and tools. Sometimes UX is not the best option. You need to know this so that you know when to back down, or when to support other people. UX isn't the only tool out there and it isn't a perfect way to get things done. Push the boundaries but know your place. Your chances of success will improve if you have a broad view of the organization and who is doing what.

Structure and Organization Pave the Road to Success

This chapter is not about throwing in the towel; quite the contrary. I'm going to help you decide exactly what to focus on if you lack a plan of action. I'll also give you a sense of what has highest priority right now, although I'll be the first to admit every situation is going to be different. Nevertheless, I feel there are some UX truisms that you can take to the bank.

First and foremost you must know your value. I'm not talking about justifying the work that you do. Instead, I'm talking about having a deep sense of your value to the organization. It's knowing in your gut that you're doing the right thing for yourself and the company. If you don't have a firm grasp on your value and your skills, you need to take action. This grounding is essential for success in any job, but especially as a usability professional.

Think of the one thing that you can provide that no one else in your company can provide. Or, if others do provide it, how can you still be number one in the eyes of those around you. Here's an example. I know a software engineer at a Fortune 100 company. He's a good engineer but that's not why people come to him. You see, he's the graphics guy. Out of all the software engineers in the entire organization he's the guy who can create charts, icons, logos, and the like. In short his brand is the "graphics guy," all while being a high quality software engineer. My point is that he has a brand and he's built a reputation. You should strive to do exactly the same thing. Brand yourself!

Brainstorming for Your Brand

If you're having trouble developing your brand it's time for some brainstorming. You're probably blind to your real skills and talents. For this reason, I suggest taking another look at your resume. What really stands out? What makes you unique? In comparison to other usability professionals – if there are any – what sets you apart from the herd?

In addition to your resume, you ought to reach out beyond your organization. For example, read some usability blogs (e.g., WebWord. com) and see if anything stands out. Look for uniqueness. Look for that special edge.

Hit various job postings on job boards. Look at what other usability professionals are saying about themselves. Find new words and phrases that capture your skills and talents. Similarly, ask other people for their resumes. You might find some interesting tidbits. Of course you can look inside your company as well. You might find something that fits really well and augments your own resume.

When brainstorming look for uniqueness because ultimately you're trying to develop a unique selling proposition or USP. The USP is the one thing that makes you unique when compared to everyone else. This is the core of your brand.

Survival of the Fittest

Whether you like it or not you're competing for scarce resources in your organization. Although money does shake free from time to time as I discussed in a previous chapter, in most cases there isn't enough money to go around. In fact, usability specialists frequently feel financial pressure. They feel marginalized and they feel like they are teetering on the brink of disaster when money isn't flowing.

Even if you feel very safe and secure in your position I encourage you to recognize that there is a war for funding. Since money is the name of the game in business, you need to find ways to position your self and your UX peers so they can withstand funding pressures.

Your Unique Selling Proposition

It is exactly for this reason that you need a unique selling proposition. It's also why I've stressed repeatedly in this book that you must map your skills and talents to the needs of the organization, and your ability to have an impact on the bottom line.

Realize that many people who are less talented are better positioned in your organization. That's because they've done an effective job in the war for recognition, which is the twin brother of the war for funding. If you've really been paying attention, you'll realize that in many chapters I've been strongly encouraging you to build a strong social network in your organization. It's this network which keeps you safe though rough times but it's also your avenue to funding and recognition. It's glue for usability professionals and their value to the bottom line.

Use What Works

I encourage you to exploit the tools and methods that other successful people in your organization employ. For example, many software developers put together libraries of software design patterns. They also create reusable libraries for other developers and even designers to exploit.

Take a chapter out of their playbook. Create easy-to-use usability testing patterns. Develop simple templates for others to do their own UX review work. Of course, offer to provide direct assistance. Make yourself available for more in-depth professional deep dives.

You Swim with a School of Fish, You're Not a Whale

I'll wrap up by emphasizing that you should never view your work in isolation. Even when you're on a project team remember that there are many other projects and priorities in your organization.

It's imperative to recognize that someone or some group has invested in your work and they expect a return on their investment. It's your duty to know your customers. You must make it a priority to know where the money came from and who provided it to you. Their butt is on the line; help them, protect them, succeed for them.

To best understand the investments others have made in you, I suggest that you spend time at the start of each project developing success metrics. Know exactly how you're being measured and what constitutes mission success. If you or your team falls off track, simply refer to the project goals. Further, reference the list of things that must be accomplished in order to be victorious.

You can also create your own personal success metrics. I encourage you to align these personal metrics to things that ultimately drive a great user experience. This connects your success to the success of customers. At the same time, the project metrics and goals connect the project itself to the company's bottom line. This weaves a strong web that improves the project and your UX career.

Summary of infiltration tips

- Never work without having a prioritized list and concrete goals.
- Know your value; tie your skills to the project and bottom line.
- You're in a war for money and attention; develop a strong USP.
- Borrow and steal what works; develop UX libraries and patterns.
- Reward the people who fund you by doing outstanding work; demonstrate ROI by surprising and delighting customers.

37

Sell! You Are Always On Display, You Are Always Selling

Freedom is just chaos, with better lighting.
~ Alan Dean Foster

What is necessary to change a person is to change his
awareness of himself.
~ Abraham H. Maslow

Summary

By now you've learned that your role in the organization can be subtle or very prominent. In general, however, you have to always be turned on and ready to go. Opportunities are everywhere. At the same time, consider that others always have you under the microscope. Be prepared, be ready. You should now understand that you are in sales. You are in marketing. You are a promotion machine which means you are on the front line at some level or another. Your customers are your peers and your management.

You're Now a Peacock on Display

Your ability to sell is paramount to your success as a usability professional. And just like a salesperson, you've got to be fired up and ready to go in the blink of an eye. At a moment's notice you need to have all pistons firing in your engine. Although this might be tough for some slow-n-steady UX'ers, being fast on your feet will bring you great rewards. It's all part of your infiltration training.

In previous chapters I've talked about always being on display and being a UX emissary. You are being judged and managing perceptions is all part of the game.

It isn't hard to beat someone to the draw if you've practiced, prepared your elevator speech, and understand whom you're talking to. Everyone in your organization is a potential customer. The bottom line is that you're in sales now. Embrace this idea to succeed!

Three Themes

I've built a salesperson persona for you. It isn't 100% accurate or complete, but it's exactly what you need to see. Drink deeply!

First, all great salespeople are entertainers. They know how to work a crowd for maximum effect. They make eye contact, firmly shake hands, and offer up a genuine smile. But most of all, they're able to tell interesting and informative stories. They'll do this in the context of your needs and desires, and there will be a punchline about business success. In particular, they know how to tell story so that you can envision your own business success.

Second, great salespeople develop associations and affiliations. They find ways to connect themselves to you. That's why they talk about sports with most men, but they talk about family and children with most women. Knock that if you wish, it works. They become likable simply by asking questions and letting you talk. They will listen very closely as you spill the beans. If you're complaining they'll offer helpful advice or encourage you to keep talking to let it all out. It's this kind of connection that they then leverage into a casual soft sell. In short, being genuine is a marketing weapon and they know it.

Third, great salespeople tend to simplify and magnify. A very easy way to do this is by using common knowledge and everyday scenarios. For example, if you want to talk about usability, all you really need to do is talk about Google or Apple. You can talk about their cultures, leaders, market share, internal processes, and then usability. By talking about Google and Apple, you're giving yourself credibility through association and by sharing a common experience with the person you're talking to. Everyone knows Google and Apple, right? Sneaking in a couple of points about usability is as easy as falling off a log because they've simplified and magnified what matters.

UX Culture Patterns Mark Success

You might be wondering how to know how you're doing as a UX salesperson in your organization. Daniel Szuc, Paul Sherman and I have stated that there are markers or "culture patterns" that indicate UX growth. For example, management is using the language of usability, the company has hired a director or VP of UX, usability testing of products is a given, product managers claim that UX is a strategic advantage, and so on. In short, other people are talking about UX not just you. They are selling for you.

You can use culture patterns to develop your own metrics. If you're going to sell UX then you have to benchmark and measure your progress. Even if you do this casually it's worth your time and effort. You want to know if your investment is paying off, or if you need to find different tactics. Marketing requires consistent and constant evolution.

I suggest that you ask yourself a number of questions as a UX salesperson. What's the number one need of your business and how does it UX apply to that need? Who is funding UX in your business right now? Are you regularly working with that person or those people? Who, besides you, is telling UX success stories? What's the number one objection to UX? Answer these questions and you're on your way to developing your sales plan.

Your Optimal Selling Strategy

If you're having trouble developing your sales plan I'm going to save you some time and energy. Here's exactly how to develop your optimal selling strategy. This is based on the work of several millionaire marketers but I specifically like how Michael Masterson has laid it out. He presents a four step plan which comes from Ready, Fire, Aim.

Your first question is, who are your customers? Note: In this context when I say "customers" I'm talking about your internal customers, like product managers and executives. Where do you find them? Who are your targets? Who are you selling to?

You don't want to try to sell UX to everyone, you want to focus as much as possible. Think about establishing a strong rapport with these people, befriending them, persuading them, and delivering helpful messages on a regular basis.

Your second question is, what's the first thing you're going to sell them? There are many different things you could offer to your internal customers. But if you try to sell too much to one person they'll get confused, and rightfully so.

When people are buying they desire simplicity. That's why it's imperative that you know the number one pain point of the business and for that individual. You're going to use that knowledge to align your UX skills to the problem and eliminate it as soon possible.

Your third question is, what do your internal customers need to give to you? Do they need to just give you time? Are you asking for funding or resources? Do you need a usability lab?

Think of the entire interaction in the framework of a sales process. Reflect on the exchange that's occuring between you and your internal customer. If you're solving their pain through UX in some way, what are they giving you in exchange? Be cognizant of the deal you're making so you can repeat the process and continue to evolve as a world class UX salesperson.

Your final question is, how are you going to convince them to buy what you're offering? You can't simply give someone the solution and expect them to take it. It works sometimes but your conversion rate will be lower than it could be. Here's a simple analogy. If you just hit someone with an offer it's like talking about sex before you're even on the first date. Take it easy, build a rapport, and then give the lady a rose. Maybe you'll get a kiss and a second date.

What are the emotional triggers that you can exploit to get your internal customer to buy what you're selling? What are you offering that provides so much value that would actually hurt to decline your offer? Find the emotional triggers of your customers to kick your selling into overdrive.

Only you can answer the questions above. It's your obligation to develop your own optimum selling strategy. The caveat is that if you have built a good network, you can work with them to develop your optimum selling strategy. All the user experience infiltration tactics build on each other. So, fear not! You have the tools and the framework to get the job done and succeed with your UX sales efforts.

Summary of infiltration tips

- Embrace the fact that you are a UX salesperson.
- Recognize that you're always on display; you're the UX beacon.
- Learn to shape your selling by using the UX Sales Persona.
- UX culture patterns define your UX marketing progress.
- Develop your own optimal selling strategy, then use it.

38

Imagine! You're a UX Consultant

*He that teaches us anything which we knew not before is
undoubtedly to be reverenced as a master.*
~ Samuel Johnson

*Ineffective people live day after day with unused potential.
They experience synergy only in small, peripheral ways in
their lives. But creative experiences can be produced regularly,
consistently, almost daily in people's lives. It requires enormous
personal security and openness and a spirit of adventure.*
~ Stephen R. Covey

Summary

Consultants live and die by contracts. They need to understand how businesses operate and they need to land sales, or they'll be eating scraps of food in a cardboard box. So, if you want to learn how to improve your chances of success you need learn more about successful consulting and how to be an entrepreneur. You need to learn how to take calculated risks like they do. Similarly, learn how consultants network and grow their business.

UX Consultants Are Battle Hardened

Consultants are in the business of creating customers out of thin air. Without customers and without cash flowing in, consultants cease to exist. In fact, the number one imperative for any consultant is to land sales and develop new customers. They must, or they can't pay the mortgage and put the kids through school. In short, winning new business is life-and-death for a consultant.

For this reason I greatly respect consultants. They are entrepreneurs and they're taking risks that many people in large organizations are unwilling to take. I enjoy speaking with consultants and working with them because they discuss the bottom line. They talk about business and I listen closely. Keep in mind that they are selling even when you are not. They must infiltrate from the outside, which is more difficult than your internal infiltration. They must do this to survive.

Disclaimer: In addition to working as a business analyst, webmaster, software engineer, and software engineering manager, I've done a healthy amount of my own usability consulting. So, I'm a bit biased about the rugged individualism and wonderful characteristics of consultants, especially UX consultants.

The Value of a UX Consultant to You, Personally

I suggest that you spend time talking to usability consultants whenever you can. Pick their brains and discover how they market because they live and breathe it every single day. You'll get more good advice by talking to a smart usability consultant than you ever will get by reading 20 marketing books. Pay special attention to consultants' ability to get new business and land sales. This prospecting is incredible.

You'll find that a lot of selling is done by other people for consultants, absolutely free. Word-of-mouth is typically the number one way for UX consultants land new business. Reputation is key!

Consultants also find that revenue is most easily generated by working with existing customers versus trying to develop new relationships with entirely new people and companies. The moral of the story is that you should continue to build on existing relationships since it's easier to keep these folks happy and acquire new business than find entirely new ones.

UX Jedi Training

The next time you're in a bookstore or online looking for new books to add to your library, consider picking up some books on providing professional services. That's a shorthand way of saying, pick up books that consultants read to improve their business. Not only will you think more like an entrepreneur, you'll be able to select a consultant to provide services if you happen to need usability assistance in the future.

Look for other opportunities to think differently about business. Grab a copy of Inc. magazine or Entrepreneur. Attend small business seminars, many of which are free. Take a marketing class. Think like a consultant.

Teach to Learn

As you know, the best way to learn something is to teach it. For this reason, consider teaching a design class at a local community college or university. Not only will you improve your public speaking skills, but you'll be able to build relationships. Smart people challenge your thinking and improve your ability to sell usability. Use the classroom as your laboratory. Indeed, if you're weak on some UX methods give them a try in your class. No harm, no foul.

Teaching is also a good way to find new interns. It goes without saying that colleges and universities are the perfect place to find bright and eager minds. That affords you with an opportunity for bringing user experience into your organization via internship opportunities.

There's yet another reason to be a teacher. Many consultants are able to get research done for free through universities by working with the professors. You can do the exact same thing, even though you might not be a consultant. Professors have an in-depth knowledge understanding of many topics. Learn new trends in marketing, business, arts, anthropology, sociology, and so forth, just by talking to professors and spending time on campus. Build these relationships.

How a Consultant Gets to the Moon

Consultants are good at bootstrapping. A smart consultant will take one very small idea and turn it into something larger than life. For example, here's a path a consultant might take to land an appearance on Oprah.

They might start by writing a very simple guest article or editorial in a local newspaper. Once published, they'd use that article as a bridge to land writing more articles, and perhaps even start writing a weekly or monthly column. From there, they'd parlay their articles or their column into a long piece in a magazine. They'd start local, but go national eventually. Once that foundation was developed, they'd then build relationships with newspapers, like the New York Times and the Wall Street Journal. That of course would lead to book deals and appearances on major TV networks. Bingo, they're on Oprah.

You can easily do bootstrapping in your organization. You can start small, perhaps with a simple email newsletter or brownbag lunches. From there you can talk to project teams or maybe start working with the helpdesk or customer service department on a regular basis. That in turn might lead you to talk with product managers and senior engineers, or maybe even junior executives. Eventually, by using your bootstrapping skills like a consultant, you'll be talking to the President and CEO, as well as prominent customers and suppliers.

If you always think of the work you're doing as a means to developing your own UX business, you'll start acting more like a consultant and entrepreneur. You'll see new opportunities present themselves to you just because you have the right frame of mind and perspective on how business is conducted. You'll be able to leverage relationships and even the smallest nuances in conversations that you're having each and every day.

Take Your UX Selling Vitamins Every Day

Selling UX is not difficult if you're treating it as a natural part of your job, just like a consultant does. Think about it like it's life or death and you'll empower yourself to take extraordinary action.

Don't think of selling UX as a one-time activity because that is precisely what makes it so difficult for most people. If you're not doing it on a regular basis, you'll get rusty and you'll be uncomfortable. So, practice selling UX on a daily basis and you'll be a marketing wizard and no time.

Summary of infiltration tips

- UX consultants are marketing wizards; network with them.
- Build on successful relationships first, they offer the highest ROI.
- Read what UX consultants are reading to gain new perspectives.
- Consultants bootstrap; iteratively build on your UX successes.
- Consider teaching at a local college or university because this will improve your public speaking skills and it will expose you to potential interns for your organization.

39

You! Cult(ure) Change: Make It Happen

Too often we underestimate the power of a touch, a smile, a kind word,
a listening ear, an honest compliment, or the smallest act of caring,
all of which have the potential to turn a life around.
~ Leo F. Buscaglia

Don't listen to anyone who tells you that you can't do this or that.
That's nonsense. Make up your mind, you'll never use crutches or
a stick, then have a go at everything. Go to school, join in all
the games you can. Go anywhere you want to. But never, never let
them persuade you that things are too difficult or impossible.
~ Douglas Bader

Summary

You must take an active role in the success of UX in your organization because no one else is going to do it for you. You cannot take a passive role. You are an agent of change. Whether you attempt a frontal assault or you take a more subtle approach, the key is to take repeated, structured, deliberate action. Culture changes are extremely difficult endeavors but you can make a difference. Become the quarterback or be a cheerleader, but definitely take steps forward.

You're a Leader

Culture change is a loaded term but I'm still going to use it because it captures the gist of what you're ultimately trying to do. You're trying to change the way your organization views UX. You also need to realize that changing the hearts and minds of your coworkers is your job because no one else is going to do it for you, at least not without nudging.

Although it's true that you might not get much support initially, using the infiltration tactics that I've provided to you will help you build the right relationships. That means involving the right people and focusing on what matters. Putting it another way, if you have the right people helping you, it is possible to change culture by leading your coworkers. You're the leader of the army.

Like a Sink Full of Dirty Dishes

The truth is culture change is a messy affair. This is exacerbated by the fact that user experience infiltration tactics are not meant to be direct and open. They're deliberately sneaky and opaque. That means your efforts to openly change your company culture are going to be kind of rough, but you can do it.

One thing you can do is obtain the explicitly documented objectives of your organization. Unless you work for very small organization, you're bound to find documented goals, or at least some sort of mission statement. Is the organizational culture truly reflected in what's documented or not? The answer is usually negative. Usually the real culture and belief system of an organization is unconscious, implicit, and ethereal.

If the mission or the goals are not well known by your coworkers, then you can start to alter the way people think about user experience simply by asking questions. When you ask questions you can embed material that will get people thinking about usability. As you know based on previous chapters, there is great power in simply asking questions and getting people to think. It's this thinking that will slowly but surely change the culture in your organization.

Dig right into this. Ask people really hard questions about the organization. Why do we do this or that? Who really knows what our number goal is? What's our typical customer look like and act like? By asking these questions you're getting people to talk about the real culture of the company. Of course when you do this, you can inject ideas about UX. It's easy to do that.

Creating a New Breed of UX Thinkers

One of the most direct ways to change culture is to provide training. Earlier I spoke about brown bag lunches. Not only can they be used to inject UX into the organization directly and immediately, they can also be used adjust the core values. In fact, one of your brownbag goals needs to be culture change.

Training sessions are a great way to get people thinking about usability and user experience. For example, if your department periodically provides training you can ask one or two questions during the training session that will get people thinking UX, although I'm careful not to sound like a broken record and I avoid directly complaining. Focus on the positive when possible, not the negative. Let other people complain. Take the high road.

If you do have the opportunity to do brown bag lunches or provide training, be sure to measure what you're doing. Metrics can have a profound effect on other people. For example, executives appreciate summarized data when you can generate it. Even a few good charts can make a difference in how executives think about usability. If you have data that shows the impact on the organization – especially productivity or profits – then you'll get the attention that you want.

It's this attention from the executives that can lead to sudden shifts in culture. This is in contrast to the more subtle and casual changes that you'll have at a personal level with your coworkers. When an executive swings the hammer a nail will be driven. It's your job to hand the executive the hammer, nail, and reason to swing.

Summary of infiltration tips

- Culture change only happens when you know you're a leader.
- Culture change is slow and messy but structure what you can.
- Training and education are launch pads for UX culture changes.

40

Them!
Cult(ure) Change Redux

Support bacteria - they're the only culture some people have.
~ Steven Wright

Per aspera ad astra.
~ Latin Proverb

Summary

You must know your company as well as you know yourself. This is your key to success. You must also understand the typical work patterns in your organization. These culture patterns will signal how much your organization will accept usability and user experience. To know the strength of the patterns you must measure and monitor. Don't shy away. Lastly, you must be strong. You must be confident. Selling usability and using these infiltration tactics requires a strong backbone and real confidence, even in the face of rejection. But, you can do it!

Know Thy Company

If you want to have an impact on the culture of your company then you must understand that culture. If you can influence leaders in your organization to make changes in favor of UX, then you must answer some of the questions below. These are based on ideas originally put forth by my colleague Paul Sherman; I can't claim ownership.

First, should UX be set up as its own department? If yes, where do these UX'ers report ultimately? They must report up through some part of the management chain and this will have an impact on your ability to inject changes. Keep in mind that some divisions and business units have more money and power (e.g., sales), whereas others might have more reach and direct influence over employees (e.g., human resources). Where UX'ers call "home" absolutely has an impact.

Second, should UX be folded under product management, quality, or engineering? That is, is it best to get UX deeply rooted in one business unit or another? What makes more sense for you from an infiltration perspective? This question becomes more import as your reputation grows and your results speak for you.

Third, are you liberated or constrained by senior management. For example, do executives maintain strict control over all design decisions? How many layers of approval are required before a particular UX is blessed by the executives? If your culture is more of a dictatorship than a democracy you might have to change your operations to enable culture change.

Fourth, what type of design and development does your organization follow? Do you adhere to more of a traditional waterfall software development lifecycle (SDLC)? Or, are you more nimble, following agile or extreme programming methods? If your organization is more traditional, for example, then generating change must be more calculated and clever since you'll have to work through more red tape. There's more scrutiny about process change and personalities generally are a bit more rigid.

Fifth, what is usually the most important project driver in your organization? That is, does your company typically put more weight on cost, schedule, or quality? If it's cost, then watching the budget and demonstrating ROI is key. If it's schedule, however, you might need to worry about speed to market or rapid design cycles. And if it's quality, you might need to work closely with the process engineers to reduce cycle time. These are all just examples, but the point is that knowing the weighting of the factors will help you position UX for greatest impact.

Sixth, is UX bottoms-up or top-down in your organization? In large part, this knowledge tells you who requires the most attention. If you're looking to really sneak UX into an organization but you're top-down, you might actually work closer with hands on coworkers and maybe first line managers. Again, just knowing how you're company positions UX is a key to effectively infiltrating.

Finally, is your company engineering-centric, marketing-centric, or design centric? If you're driven by engineering then you might not even really have UX in the company. The company has grown organically due to pure technical innovation and products are given attention simply because they are interesting, not because they offer an outstanding UX. Other companies are design-centric, and they focus on products that designers love. An outpouring of creativity generates products. And lastly, sales and marketing-centric organizations are pushed by a powerful sales force that claims to have perfect knowledge of customers. Although they pull in money, they are often blind to the upside potential of UX.

Hitting the Bullseye

Daniel Szuc put together a list which represents a framework for understanding the targets within your organization. In other words, the list gives you new perspectives on your internal customers.

I'll get to the list in a moment. Before I do that, please consider the importance of knowing your customer. If you don't have a clear idea then you simply cannot sell. And, if you cannot sell, then you cannot drive culture change. Here's the list. I'll throw in comments along the way.

First, is the person you're targeting in management? More importantly, do they have power and influence? Are they leaders and can they affect change? Although you never know who will help you, leadership has the greatest ability to drive culture change in the shortest period of time.

Second, is the person an existing UX champion? In a previous chapter I indicated that it's best to target people who already know the true value of UX. But there's more here. The champion might have a high, medium or low interest. They might be tactical and focused on the current business quarter, or they might have a long term strategic vision. Further, this champion might be thinking of how UX can help them professionally, perhaps through major project success or maybe a promotion due to outstanding customer feedback. These people would be champions due to your ability to assist them with UX methods and systems.

Third, your targets might be influenced by the current morale situation. For example, maybe you're organization is facing incredible market pressure. Perhaps your company is considering layoffs and your coworkers are looking for special assistance. Remember the UX sometimes can be a silver bullet. This isn't always the case but the point is that you might find the some people become more receptive to UX when they are faced with uncertainty, pressure, or stress. UX offers a surprising amount of certainty.

Recognize that there are various reasons why your internal customers would be warm or cold to UX. If you understand the basic framework above, you can sell better. If you can sell better then you'll be able to more effectively inject UX into your organization.

User Experience Culture Patterns

I've repeatedly encouraged you to collect and analyze data. When you measure something, you can understand it better and control it.

For this reason, you should take a look at the UX culture patterns all around you. Your organization is at some level of UX maturity and there are markers that I'm going to provide below.

You know that you've hit the UX jackpot when...

First, you hear managers and executives using UX lingo. Of course, they might not say "pluralistic walkthrough" but they might be talking a lot more about customer satisfaction, smart design, easy-to-use products, and so forth. You have to pay close attention since attitude changes might be happening, even if the language isn't changing.

Second, the company has hired new UX'ers. These folks might be interns or day-to-day works like junior usability engineers, or they might have hired a Director or VP of UX. If your company has brought in these folks, you know that UX is getting in deep. The culture has changed, without a shadow of a doubt.

Third, usability testing is a "given" in the company. It's just something that is always done because the value is so high but also so obvious to everyone. You might even have a fully funded usability lab.

Finally, product managers, engineers, and marketing all claim that UX offers a strategic advantage for the company. For example, UX might always be part of strategic conversations, perhaps in reference to new products and services coming to market.

If you see these culture patterns you know that UX has become important to your organization. The need to justify UX goes down. And, your need to use some of the more sneaky UX infiltration tactics likewise decreases. You can be more open and frank about UX, although some tactics will never go out of style. For example, being generous and patient will always win you points. Further, if you can continue to improve your presentation skills, writing skills, and listen skills, you'll continue to grow as a usability professional.

Here's why you want to watch culture patterns. If someone else demonstrates a positive impact to the bottom line you will never have to sell or justify UX again. So, keep looking for those culture patterns and keep driving change in your organization. Use the UX infiltration tactics as much as needed to get the job done.

Confidence My Friend, Have Confidence!

I'll end with this. If you haven't convinced yourself of the value of usability and user experience then you'll never have the confidence or the ability to enable culture change in your organization. You must truly believe in the work that you do. You must know that you're an emissary for UX. You'll be amazed at your ability to change the very core of your organization if you believe in yourself.

I encourage you to step away from your day job for a moment and reflect. You now have an incredible toolbox of user experience infiltration tactics. Bind UX tactics to the right attitude and you can make a difference.

If you take what I've said to heart, change will happen. You'll hardly be selling UX at all since others will sell it for you. They'll flock to you, begging for help and you'll be there for them.

Embrace the change. Become the change.
It's now within your reach.

Summary of infiltration tips

- Be sure to very clearly understand your corporate culture.
- Know your internal customers well before you target them.
- Always be looking for UX culture patterns; use measurements.
- Have confidence in your culture changing abilities; you can do it!

Index